The Book of Haughley

At the Heart of Suffolk

WRITTEN BY THE MEMBERS OF
THE HAUGHLEY LOCAL HISTORY FORUM

*COMPILED AND EDITED BY
CELIA AND HOWARD STEPHENS
AND COLIN HART*

HALSGROVE

First published in Great Britain in 2005

Copyright © 2005 Celia and Howard Stephens

All rights reserved. No part of this publication may be reproduced, stored in a retrieval system, or transmitted in any form, or by any means without the prior permission of the copyright holder.

British Library Cataloguing-in-Publication Data.
A CIP record for this title is available from the British Library.

ISBN 1 84114 416 9

Halsgrove

Halsgrove House
Lower Moor Way
Tiverton, Devon EX16 6SS
Tel: 01884 243242
Fax: 01884 243325
Email: sales@halsgrove.com
Website: www.halsgrove.com

Title page photograph: *The Post Mill in Station Road, 1938.*

Printed and bound in Great Britain by CPI Bath.

Whilst every care has been taken to ensure the accuracy of the information contained in this book, the publisher disclaims responsibility for any mistakes which may have been inadvertently included.

Preamble

This book has been compiled by the members of the Haughley Local History Forum. It has been very much a team effort and, although some names appear as the authors of individual chapters, it was only through the combined efforts of the whole group that this book has come to fruition. Those who have helped in the research, collation and editing are:

Gerard Artingdale, Geoff Clarke, David Fleetwood, Bill Green, Colin Hart, Sue Moore, Fred Rapsey, Dennis Spink, Celia Stephens, Howard Stephens, Dennis Urban, Marion Wilson.

Acknowledgements

The Members of the Haughley Local History Forum would like to acknowledge the support they have received from so many people in the village. To all those who took the time to come along and tell their stories, identify faces in ancient photographs, lend us photographs and cuttings and generally contribute to our efforts we extend our warmest thanks. Without your help this book would not have been possible. We would like in particular to record our appreciation to Richard Coe for access to his amazing archive of photos and cuttings, Ken Palmer for permission to use photographs from his collection, Robert Williams for permission to use his history of Haughley Park, Maurice Hart for his amazing memory, Alex and James Bevan for access to their family archives, and the many people who have opened up their archives and photograph collections for us.

In researching and collecting photographs for this book the group has tried to trace original sources. It is, however, a complicated business, especially with the photographs. There are many copies of the same pictures in existence. Sometimes postcards seem to have been produced from earlier photographs, at other times it appears that the postcard negative has been used to produce some further prints. It is almost impossible to tell which came first. Wherever possible permission has been sought to use the photographs from what we believe is the original source. However, the book is produced for the benefit of the village and not as a profit-making venture (any net income will be distributed to village charities), so if we have inadvertently used someone's photographs without permission and acknowledgement, we crave your understanding.

Revd Nigel MacCulloch started his book *Haughley Past and Present* with an apology, if parts of the book were to be found boring. He quoted Richard Steele in the *Tatler Number 38:* 'It is to be noted that where any part of this paper is dull there is design in it.'

We hope that you will not find this book dull and that the pictures and recollections will spark off happy memories of Haughley. We have enjoyed writing it and, although we would have to admit to times when we recalled the *Syrus maxim* 'Be careful about starting something you may regret', we took immediate solace from Horace's *Epistulatae*: 'Nulla placere diu nec vivere carmina possunt quae scribuntur aquae potoribus' – 'Water drinkers don't make good writers!'

We also sincerely hope that we have not upset anyone along the way, for as Cicero said, 'to write without clarity and charm is a miserable waste of time and ink.' We make no claim to this being a definitive history of the village, for it is not. Our aim is to capture some of those moments in the life of Haughley and its folk that set our village apart and make it a place from which almost all are reluctant to leave.

Contents

Preamble   3

Acknowledgements   4

Chapter One	The History of Haughley	7
Chapter Two	Dwellings and Domestic Life	19
Chapter Three	Haughley at Work	39
Chapter Four	Haughley at War	53
Chapter Five	The Church of the Assumption of the Blessed Virgin Mary	63
Chapter Six	Transport in Haughley	81
Chapter Seven	Farming in Haughley	97
Chapter Eight	Local Characters and Their Stories	107
Chapter Nine	Village Organisations and Celebrations	119
Chapter Ten	Looking to the Future	153

Subscribers   157

Further Titles   159

Above: *Looking east from the church tower, c.1970.*

Left: *The moat and Duke Street in the 1940s.*

Below: *An aerial view of the village from the south west in the mid-1960s, with the grain silo and Haughley Junction Station in the distance.*

Chapter One
The History of Haughley
Celia and Howard Stephens

Haughley has a varied history. There is evidence of it being a thriving market town in medieval times, but its position on high ground made it difficult to serve by railway. Since the coming of the railway to Suffolk, the importance of the village declined and it is often quoted that 'from the ruins of Haughley Stow arose.' In truth the decline started somewhat before the age of steam. Although there were the Dagger Docks at Dagworth, the Gipping was really only regularly navigable to Stowmarket. A fire in the early-eighteenth century, the discontinuation of the early market and the ending of the annual toy fair in 1871, all point to a gradual shift away from Haughley towards Stowmarket, taking place over a few hundred years. Nevertheless, Haughley in the early-twenty-first century is an expanding and lively village with a proud history. In this and the following chapters we hope to capture some of the moments that have changed life in Haughley and have moulded it into the pleasant and bustling community that it is.

The Village Name

On the ancient maps Haughley appears in several different forms – Hawley, Hawleigh, Haughleigh – and it would be reasonable to assume that the name simply means the 'The field with the Hawthorn tree', or something very similar. However, in a will dated 1040 the village was called Hagela and in the Domesday Book of 1080 it was spelt Hagala. In the Charter Rolls of 1247 it was spelt Haggle, in the Pipe Rolls of 1165 it was called Hagenet and in the 1254 Book of Fees it was called Haule. There are over 40 different spellings in the ancient records. This is not surprising because names were rarely written and were mostly passed on by word of mouth.

At first glance it seems that the word might come from the old English 'haga', which means a haw or hawthorn, and so our first guess might be right. This would be appropriate in an area where the Hawthorn grows in plenty and there are other local villages that take their names from trees (Ashfield, Elmswell, Walsham-le-Willows). Unfortunately, there was an identical old English word 'haga' which meant a fenced enclosure and, since we know that there was a castle at Haughley from early times, this also seems to be a reasonable meaning of the name. If that were not complicated enough, there was also an old English word 'haugh' which was a mound or hillock, perhaps the one on which the castle sits. The fact is that we shall probably never know for sure and you may take your pick!

Throughout this book we shall talk of Haughley and sometimes we shall be meaning the village and other times the whole parish. From the earliest records that exist the parish of Haughley has retained its basic form. It is the shape of an inverted 'Y' with the village of Haughley on the junction of the three arms, with Haughley Green to the north, Haughley New Street and Haughley Park to the bottom left and Tothill to the bottom right. As with much of Suffolk the area would once have been forest and many of the natural routes followed the watercourses. Haughley sits near the source of a tributary of the Gipping (from which Gipperswick, now Ipswich, takes its name) and is only a few miles from the Suffolk watershed, beyond which the land drains to the north-west towards King's Lynn.

One of our previous vicars, Revd Nigel MacCulloch, compiled a history of the village which was published in 1983, and in this book we do not intend to cover the same ground, but to present a series of snapshots of Haughley over the years. However, it is necessary to set the parish in its historical context so we shall start with a quick look at the history.

Pre-Conquest History

Because of the lack of records, little is known of Haughley before the Norman Conquest, so we have to make some assumptions based on what was happening in the region at the time. Prior to the Romans arriving in Britain, the inhabitants were a comparatively uncivilised race, but the early steps towards a civilised society started in East Anglia. The religion was Druidism, probably introduced by the Phoenicians from Cadiz, who were the first significant traders and merchants to visit Britain. As trade developed and encompassed other regions in Britain, tin became an important commodity – it was partly due to the wish to track down the source of the tin that the Romans came to Britain.

The Druid tribe that dwelt in our area of East Anglia was the Iceni and the region was known as Cenomanni or Ceniomagni. The Iceni came to Britain from present-day France in about 1000BC and a few traces of their existence can still be found in names such as Icnield Street and Iksning, that became Exning.

The Romans first came to England under Julius Caesar in 55BC but this adventure did not bring them in any number to East Anglia because civil war in Rome meant that the army was recalled. In AD43 Emperor Claudius sent an army under the command of Plautius and it was this invasion, subsequently led by Suetonius Paulinus, that was to achieve the conquest of Britain. The Druids fiercely resisted the Roman invasion and there were many bloody battles; it was only after the defeat of Boudicca that the Iceni were subdued and Roman rule was imposed in the area.

We know from their histories and from the pattern of the older roads that the Romans settled in the immediate area of Haughley. They had established the town of Colchester and the main route though the Haughley area would not have been the east–west route that we have today, but the road from Colchester, possibly via an ancient settlement at Claydon and on to Ixworth and eventually to King's Lynn, Lincoln and northwards.

In his 1880 *History of Stowmarket* Hollinsworth asserted that the Roman town of Sitomagus was at Haughley, but others place it at Dunwich, Thetford, Woolpit or Ixworth (which seems more likely). However, there have been a few Roman finds in the area and it seems possible that there was a Roman camp, possibly on the site now occupied by the castle and the Folly. The word 'Folly' may well be derived from the Latin '*Vallum*', meaning the wall or rampart around the edge of the encampment, or it may derive from a later Norman French word 'Fouillé', meaning a ditch and rampart from the days when we know there was a Norman castle here. Beyond the speculation, the first concrete reference we have was in a will dated around 1040, when a lady by the name of Leofgifu left the parish to her daughter Aelfflad. After that there was reference to the parish or manor belonging to Guthmund of Stanstead. Guthmund was of Danish descent; was a minor member of the royal household and the brother of Wulfric, the Abbot of Ely. Wulfric granted him various estates in Norfolk and Suffolk to enhance his brother's chances of winning the hand of the daughter of Earl Wulfgar of East Anglia. By acquiring these lands he attained the rank of 'thane' (a freeman granted land by the king in return for military service in Anglo-Saxon England, and a man ranking above an ordinary freeman and below a nobleman). In response to his duties as a thane, he found himself at Hastings to try to fend off the Norman invasion. Unfortunately he suffered the same fate as King Harold and was killed in the battle.

The 'Honor' of Haughley

From this point onwards the history becomes easier to trace, but before we go further it might be as well to explain a couple of the terms that are used frequently throughout the records. An 'honor' was a senior lordship. It was a highly noble and prestigious award and gave authority over a number of minor lordships. These lesser positions were granted in return for the provision of knights, soldiers and archers to fight for the King when necessary. A 'constable' was the person appointed to hold a castle for the King. A 'manor' (from the old French 'manoire') was the principal dwelling-house in the estate, where the lord lived, hence the expression 'lord of the manor'. The term was later expanded by usage to mean the house and the associated estates. The lord of the manor usually split the estates into two distinct parts: one to support himself and the other, larger part, to let out to tenants in return for military and financial support.

William the Conqueror presented the 'Honor of Haughley', together with other estates, to Hugh de Montfort as reward for his part in the conquest. Hugh came from Montfort-sur-Risle in Eure, Normandy. He was also made Constable of Dover and Haughley became an 'honor constabulairie' – a lordship with an integrated castle of which the lord of the 'honor' would be constable. This meant that Haughley was regarded

Old Street in the 1890s.

as a royal estate of some seniority and importance and, although it was granted to successive lords of the manor it could and did always revert to the Crown. Thus, from this point onwards the manor remained in the control and gift of the Crown for some 850 years.

Hugh was killed in a duel with Walcheline de Ferrers and the manor passed to his son, also Hugh. This was the first of many changes of ownership that resulted from such turbulent times. When William II came to the throne he was challenged by his brother Robert, Duke of Normandy. Hugh junr sided with Robert, but when the challenge petered out and King William remained on the throne, the manor was confiscated by the Crown and Hugh departed on a crusade from which he never returned.

There is then some doubt, but it appears that the honour was granted to Robert de Vere who had married Hugh's sister, Adeline, and became King's Constable in about 1151. When he died the manor was held briefly by Gilbert de Gant, Earl of Lincoln, but he died in 1156 and the honour passed to Henry of Essex, who was Constable of England and the King's standard-bearer. Henry would have seen little of his property. He accompanied the King in the battles against the Welsh in 1157 and by 1159 was 'fighting valiantly' at Toulouse. However, Robert de Montfort labelled him a traitor and challenged him to trial by battle at Fry's Island on the River Thames near Reading. This took place on 18 April 1163 and Henry was beaten and assumed to be dying. He was taken to Reading Abbey where he did eventually recover, but the manor was again forfeited to the Crown.

Later that year the King allowed Robert Fitz Isilie and later Ralph of Rochester, William de Assheford and Robert de Wells to occupy the manor. When Richard II came to the throne he gave the manor to Count Thomas de Perche when the Count married the niece of Richard the Lionheart, Matilda of Saxony. Count Thomas was killed at the Fair of Lincoln in 1218 and Haughley Manor was amongst his possessions that yet again reverted to the Crown.

Hubert de Burgh was granted the manor shortly afterwards and was made constable in 1227. It was he who obtained a charter to hold a market in the village, the royal assent of Henry III being given in 1231. Market Street was the former name of Duke Street and one can imagine that the market took place around the village green, with stalls in the area where Palmer's Bakery now stands. The charter for the market is relatively early and certainly predates Stowmarket and others in the immediate area. It was therefore the cause of a number of problems with outside traders setting up their stalls on the approach roads to the village to try to capture the trade. Several successful prosecutions are recorded against butchers from Stowmarket, and one against a William Hoxon who was 'lying in wait near the town'.

In 1235 Richard Earl of Cornwall, the brother of Henry III, King of the Romans and Lord of Eye, had

The moat from the church tower.

been granted the honour. It was during this period that a close connection was set up with Hailes Abbey in Gloucestershire. In 1242 Richard had survived a shipwreck and in thanksgiving he founded the Abbey of Hailes. He then endowed the abbey with income from Haughley and gave the Abbot of Hailes the right to appoint the vicars at Haughley. This right stayed with the Abbot until the reign of Henry VIII and the Dissolution of the Monasteries. Hailes Abbey was destroyed in 1539 and the right to appoint the vicars passed temporarily to the lord of the manor. Richard and his wife, Countess Isabella Marshall, certainly stayed at Haughley, the records state in the castle, but, as we shall see later, the castle had already been destroyed in 1173, so it is more likely that they stayed in a house that stood where Castle Farm now stands, within the former inner bailey of the original castle. Isabella gave birth to a son, Henry, at Haughley on 12 November 1235. Henry was christened in Haughley church in the following January. His father Richard was crowned King of the Romans at Aachen on 17 May 1257 and the next day he knighted his son as Henry of Almayne. Henry was another who met a violent death. He was murdered in the Church of San Lorenzo at Viterbo in Italy. His assailants were his cousins, Simon and Guy de Montfort, who were taking revenge for the death of their father Simon de Montfort at the Battle of Evesham. It was during Henry's holding of the honour that the first known vicar of Haughley was appointed. The church records show that this was John de Monte Luelli, probably an Italian. His was the first name in a list of vicars that can be traced without a break to the present day.

The manor then appears to have passed to Henry's son Edmund, but he died in 1300 and the manor once

Above: *Looking south-east from the church tower, over the Village Hall to Haughley House.*

Left: *The Folly in 1953. The line of the Folly followed the line of the outer bailey to Haughley Castle, and the ground falls quite sharply away from the Folly on the west and south sides.*

Below: *Looking north-east from the church tower and out across the King George V Playing Field.*

again reverted to the Crown. The records then become a little confusing but it seems that the King granted the manor for a short period to Gilbert de Risshton, but by the following year the income from the manors of Haughley and Eye were granted to support Margaret, the Countess of Cornwall and the widow of Edmund. However, a contradictory record suggests that in 1316 both manors were granted to another Margaret, Margaret de Clare, the King's niece.

By this time the lord of the manor had the right of 'oyer and terminer', which meant that he could hear and pass judgement on criminal cases. A gallows, for the more serious offences, was erected at the expense of the Abbot of Hailes, and was placed on Lubberlow Field, just beyond the site of today's picnic area. At the time of writing the field is still named as Gallows Field on the Ordnance Survey maps.

In 1319 King Edward II granted the manor to his Queen, Isabella, who held it until 1330 when it was granted to the King's brother John of Eltham, Earl of Cornwall. John appointed Walter Faucoun as custodian of the manor, along with the manor of Eye and the villages of Aldeton, Dallinghoo and Thorndon. John died in 1336 and in the following year the manor passed to Robert de Ufford, Earl of Suffolk. His son William inherited the manor and held it until his death in 1382 (some records say 1384). His widow, Isabel, continued to hold the manor for a while but in 1385 Richard II granted it to Michael de la Pole on the basis that although he could take an income from the manor, he could not actually take possession until Isabel died. In contrast with many in the story so far, Isabel was long-lived and survived until 1416. The manor passed from one de la Pole to another as battles, various misfortunes and beheadings overtook them. Eventually the line died out, when Edmund de la Pole, fighting for the French against the Holy Roman Emperor, was executed.

In 1510 Sir John Heydon had been appointed as custodian of the manor and keeper of Haughley Park for as long as Edmund lived (one Thomas Belle had held the post for a year previously). When Edmund was killed in 1513 it was given to his widow Margaret de la Pole for life, but this turned out to be just two years, and then, in 1515, Sir Thomas Tyrell was appointed keeper of Haughley Park and lord of the manor. He was succeeded by Charles Brandon, Duke of Suffolk, in 1527. He was brother-in-law to Henry VIII, but he opted to exchange the manor for other estates and the Crown then granted the manor to Andrew Sulyard. The Sulyards lived at Wetherden Hall, which was a fine house where, in 2005, Wetherden Hall Farm now stands. The manor stayed in the Sulyard family for over 300 years.

The grant of the manor was confirmed by Queen Mary when she came to the throne. John Sulyard, still based at Wetherden Hall, had been captain of her bodyguard and a loyal supporter. There were a few interruptions – for some reason the grant was withdrawn in February 1556 but was re-granted in the November of that year. His son's inheritance of the title was unsuccessfully challenged and then during the Civil War and subsequent Commonwealth the manor was confiscated because the Sulyards had been strong Royalists. However, the grant was reinstated at the Restoration.

In 1811 there were just three female descendants of the Sulyard line who were the joint heiresses of the manor and Haughley Park, and they sought royal permission to sell up. This was granted for a fee of £3,000 and the manor was bought by John Hayward for some £27,840 – an extraordinary amount of money in those days. At this time the estate consisted of 2,442 acres, 22 dwelling-houses, 28 messuages (dwellings with some ground and outbuildings), the mansion, farms and other supporting offices, and parkland of a further 396 acres. Hayward later sold it to Mr Joseph Beaumont and he broke up the estates and sold them off piecemeal. In 1922 the lordship was bought by Mr Gibson Jarvie. He died and the lordship was then bought by Robin de la Lenne Mirlees who sold it on to Richmond Herald.

In 1977 Jeffrey Bowden, by then already living in Haughley House, bought the lordship and has retained the title ever since.

Much of the remaining early history of which we know revolves around the castle and the main houses of Haughley.

The Castle

For those interested in further information, the history of the castle has been described in some detail in a booklet by Kieron Palmer. It is difficult to be precise about the castle's history prior to the twelfth century, but as already mentioned it could quite possibly have been the site of a Roman camp. From the air the lines of the motte (the mound and tower) and baileys can be seen clearly. The castle in its strongest form was probably built by the Norman holders of the manor after the conquest. Prior to then there was no great history of castles in England and it was the Normans who built up a network of routes and castles to help them complete the conquest of England. The castle would then have consisted of a strong tower erected on a high mound and surrounded by a moat, with inner and outer ramparts, probably capped with wooden fencing. The tower would have been the main defensive part of the castle, to which the garrison would have retreated if forced to do so, but the main living quarters would have been in the inner bailey and the outer bailey would have housed the peasants and cattle.

There is some confusion in the records and amongst those later interpreting them. Most accounts say that the castle was destroyed in 1173 and was not rebuilt. The most likely history is that after 1173 the castle within the inner bailey was

An aerial photograph of Haughley showing Old Street and the Folly. The circular nature of the Folly reflects the former outer bailey to the castle. The photograph was taken in the mid-1960s, when the houses in Castle Rise and Church View were under construction.

Right: *Ducks on the moat, c.1910.*

Below: *Castle Farm, which stands in the former inner bailey of the castle and occupies the site of a larger manor-house, probably dating from the rebuilding in the twelfth or thirteenth century.*

rebuilt, but without the keep. There was no other known major house in the manor at that time and it is inconceivable that the distinguished list of lords of the manor would have held the manor and spent time here without a house of some substance. Thus we can imagine a fortified manor-house, probably sitting where Castle Farmhouse sits in 2005. There has also been some debate over the structure of the keep, some believing that it was simply a wooden tower. In the Suffolk Record Office an eighteenth-century manuscript (SRO (B) HB502/8/23) describes the keep as having been built with flints and wrought freestone. Richard Ray Esq., who then lived at Plashwood, had great difficulty in removing the stones because the cement was as hard as the stone itself. But he succeeded in flattening the base, leaving the stone foundations level with the top of the mound, as they remain to this day. At the base, the motte was about 210 feet in diameter and this rose up in a conical shape for some 80 feet to the stone keep on the top. This in itself was some 80 feet in diameter and may have been a further 40 or 50 feet tall. The walls of the keep were 8 feet thick.

The earliest mention of the castle comes from the first half of the twelfth century. Empress Matilda granted Hugh Bigod an earldom to try to win his allegiance in the Civil War with Stephen. Although it was commonly known as the Earldom of Norfolk, Bigod's title was correctly known as the Earldom of East Anglia, since it included Suffolk. Henry I had given the 'Honor' of Eye and his castles at Eye, Haughley and Bury St Edmunds to Stephen and so prevented Bigod from gaining control of West Suffolk.

By the beginning of Henry II's reign there were no castles in royal hands in Suffolk. Hugh Bigod held Bungay, Framlingham and Walton (and Thetford in Norfolk). But Henry was concerned about the rivalry between Hugh Bigod and another great baron of the time, William de Blois. The weakness of the royal power in East Anglia led Henry to confiscate all their castles in 1157, although Framlingham and Bungay were returned in 1165 when William de Blois died. His 'Honor' of Boulogne and its associated estates passed to the Crown and this gave Henry legitimate control over Eye and Haughley Castles. He then began to build Orford Castle in 1166.

During the war of 1173/74 between Henry and his sons, one of their rebel supporters, Robert Earl of Leicester, went to France on the pretence of going to the King's assistance. In fact he joined forces with the King's son and, after a failed attempt at peace, he brought a force of Flemings over to England. They landed on 29 September at Walton in Suffolk where they knew they had the support of Hugh Bigod. They decided to bypass the impressive Orford Castle, but the combined forces of Robert and Bigod marched on Haughley and set siege to the castle on 9 October. The castle was defended by Ralph de Broc (who had been the administrator of Canterbury during the exile of Thomas à Becket). He had a small compliment of 30 knights. They held out for four days but were eventually driven out by smoke and fire. The castle was taken and destroyed. The knights were ransomed and the remainder of the garrison, probably in the order of 120 men, would have been removed and killed. The rebels then moved on to relieve Leicester, Robert's own castle, which was being besieged, but they were halted at Fornham St Genevieve by Richard de Lucie, Humphrey de Bohun, the Constable and the Earls of Cornwall, Gloucester and Arundel. The Flemings were completely routed and Robert and his wife captured. In 1174 Bigod captured Norwich Castle but was later forced to submit to Henry and was required to give up all his castles. Framlingham, his main stronghold, was destroyed, as were the castles at Bungay and Walton.

After 1173, although there are several references to Haughley Castle (including it being the birthplace of Henry Earl of Cornwall, and reference to the Uffords preferring their castle at Haughley to that at Bungay), the likelihood is that the castle was never rebuilt as a castle but that a large, possibly fortified mansion was built within the inner bailey of the castle. In a 1780 manuscript, held in the Record Office, it is recorded that:

... the inner yard, or court, of the castle; near the middle of which now stands a good farm house of no very ancient date; but where once stood a much larger building, as appeared by some of the foundations (composed of flints etc) which were dug up at the back of the present house about 45 years ago upon making a garden there. Also about 45 years ago part of the moat was cleared and sills of the drawbridge found.

Haughley Park

Haughley Park has also played a part in the history of Haughley. In the mid-fifteenth century Sir John Sulyard moved from Eye to Wetherden Hall. Sir John was a man of influence and importance and was Lord Chief Justice to Henry VII. His son Andrew became 'esquire to the body', or captain of the bodyguard of Mary Tudor, sister of Henry VII. She had been forced to marry the ageing King Louis XII of France and when he died she returned to England. Before another convenient marriage could be arranged, she married in secret her sweetheart Charles Brandon, Duke of Suffolk. Charles Brandon had exchanged the honour of Haughley for other Crown estates and so it was arranged that the lordship should be given to Andrew Sulyard.

In 1553 when Edward VII died, lady Jane Grey was declared Queen by the Protector Northumberland. Northumberland was worried about the rightful claim of Mary, Henry VIII's eldest daughter, and so pursued her. She fled to Sawston Hall near

An 1818 engraving of Haughley Park House's east façade.

Haughley Park, c.1966, after restoration by Alfred Williams.

Cambridge but that was razed when she arrived, and so she sped on to the Howard family at Kenninghall, where several of her supporters, including Andrew Sulyard's nephew John Sulyard, had gathered. John Sulyard, who had followed his uncle's profession and was captain of the bodyguard of the Princess Mary, raised a substantial escort of men and horses in Haughley and Wetherden and shepherded Mary to safety at Framlingham, where a sizeable army of over 13,000 men had been assembled. However, Northumberland's support collapsed and Mary rode to London to claim the throne.

Andrew Sulyard had died without heirs and for his support Mary confirmed the grant of the honor to Sir John Sulyard. Sir John Sulyard died in 1574 and was laid to rest in a fine tomb in Wetherden church in the aisle built by his grandfather, the Lord Chief Justice.

The Sulyards were Catholic and they were not in favour during the reign of Elizabeth, but in 1620 a third John Sulyard built the mansion in Haughley Park and it was from here that the family exercised its lordship, until the male line died out in 1799. There were three daughters – two had already married and the youngest, Frances, married George Jerningham in 1800. They lived at Haughley Park until 1809 and five of their children were born there. In 1809 George inherited the family baronetcy and moved to the family seat at Costessey. *[A comprehensive set of correspondence concerning the engagement and marriage of Frances Sulyard to George Jerningham is indexed on the web: www.adam-matthew-publications.co.uk/digital_guides]*

The Haughley Park estate was then sold in 1811 to the Crawfords (father and son) who lived there until

The north façade of Haughley Park House in 2005. The avenue leads in a straight line from the house to the church in Wetherden.

1865. They left bequests for village charities and the building of Haughley Crawford's School (and Wetherden School) and are commemorated in the churches of both villages. The Pretyman family, of which a branch lived at Bacton Manor, bought the house and lived there until 1918 when Mrs Pretyman died. It was empty for six years until purchased by Mr and Mrs Turner Henderson. He was a retired tea planter, big-game hunter and animal lover. When he died in 1956 he left the house and grounds to London Zoo for a safari park but the zoo turned it down as unsuitable. The property was then under threat of demolition when Mr Alfred Williams bought it in 1957. He had a family business that had started in Elmswell to supply eggs for Williams Brothers grocers, who operated in London from 1872 to 1973. However, the accent moved more onto poultry processing rather than eggs and the offices of the Williams family firm, John Rannoch Ltd were set up in the south end of the house.

Before the Williams family could occupy the house, it needed extensive restoration and it was during this work in 1961 that the interior of the northern part of the house was destroyed by fire. The main casualty was a magnificent Jacobean oak staircase and this was carefully replaced in oak as part of the extended restoration project. Alfred Williams was a generous man with a great interest in the local people, and particularly in the local churches of Suffolk. With the Duke of Grafton he was co-founder of the Suffolk Historic Churches Trust, an interest now continued by his son Robert Williams.

Plashwood

Another key house in the parish is Plashwood. The original property stood to the north of the Wetherden road and the present house was built in Victorian times. The house stood in what was probably the original deer park of Haughley Castle and still retains extensive park-style lands around it. The house was the property of the Ray family in the eighteenth century and their hatchments and monuments can be seen in the church. The house was purchased by the Bevan family in 1901, who ran the farm and estate associated with the property. The Bevan family are

Plashwood, 1912.

Plashwood in the 1930s.

A cartoon by Colin Hart, commenting on an attempt by the lord of the manor, Jeffrey Bowden, to restore use of the village green to its proper purpose.

another who have been generous benefactors to the village. In 1905 Wilfred Bevan was the chief benefactor in providing the Village Hall that stands in the Folly at the time of writing – previously this had been a malting in the ownership of Mr Felgate. In 1903 Wilfred Bevan donated a clock to the church, which remains in 2005. The tradition continues today with John and now and James Bevan generously allowing the use of their grounds and contributing in many ways to the well-being of the church and local charities.

Haughley House

Back in the village, the other house of significance is Haughley House, the residence of the lord of the manor in 2005, Jeffrey Bowden. The origins of this house are relatively late in the scheme of things, being built in the 1400s but with many later additions. It was obviously a new development at a time when Haughley was starting to expand, but it would not have been built as the manor-house originally, since the lords of the manor resident in Haughley lived either at Haughley Castle or Haughley Park. However, it could possibly have been built as a residence for one of the custodians of the manor, who looked after the running of the estates in the absence of the lord of the manor. It was clearly in use in Tudor times for the house has a priest's hole and there is a tunnel which, it is believed, went to the church, but is now sealed off.

Haughley House, c.1920, the residence of the lord of the manor in 2005, Jeffrey Bowden.

Still held in the house are the manorial records dating back to the thirteenth century, and a fascinating survey of the manor from 1554 that was taken at the time of Queen Mary's accession to the throne. The records include, amongst a mass of information, details of land held by Lawrence Lyng, Roger Bell, Nicholas Garnham, Alice Brett, Thomas Blowgate (there is a comprehensive website, 'Descendants of Thomas Blowgate', for anyone interested in following this family line), John Wetherby, Robert Kirby, Robert Broke and Thomas Betts. In living memory the house has been occupied by Major Creagh who took a keen interest in village life and hosted a number of events for local children and village organisations. This is again a tradition carried on by the occupants in 2005, Caroline and Jeffrey Bowden. As lord of the manor, Jeffrey Bowden has had his fair share of publicity. He is, by his own admission, an eccentric and at times an awkward character. His fights over planning permission for his flagpole or the preservation of the village green have seen his name in the papers in a less than balanced light. Behind the scenes Mr and Mrs Bowden have also contributed generously to village life through the Evergreens, the Twinning Association, the Parish Council, the Parochial Church Council and fund-raising for the church itself.

Feeding the Poor

In Tudor times a major problem for Haughley, as for most other parishes, was the maintenance of the poor. Prior to Henry VIII's Dissolution of the Monasteries the poor had largely been cared for by the abbeys, monasteries, convents and other religious houses. The disappearance of most of these coincided with a time of population growth in England and relief of the poor really became a serious problem for the first time.

At first the system relied on the generosity of those who could afford to help, but this was not successful. In the late-sixteenth century alms collectors were appointed to go from house to house seeking voluntary donations, but this was hardly more successful, and so in 1601 the Poor Law Act was introduced. This set up a compulsory tax, means tested and collected within the parish, and this paid

Looking up Old Street to the Coal House in 1993, from where coal was distributed to the poor. (PHOTOGRAPH GEOFF CLARKE)

THE HISTORY OF HAUGHLEY

Above: *Four of the fire buckets inside the church. These would have been passed from hand to hand from the moat to the scene of a fire, but one wonders how much water actually got to the fire!*

Left: *The Post Mill in Station Road, before it burnt down in 1943.*

The Folly, c.1910, before development!

for some cash relief. It also enabled the purchase of boots, clothing, fuel and simple equipment for the poor to earn their own living. The problem with this was that some parishes were better at it than others and so the poor would wander from parish to parish until they found the most favourable conditions and then settled there. This was addressed in the 1662 Poor Law Act of Settlement, which gave parishes the right to eject strays unless they could pay a basic rent or otherwise guarantee that they would not become a burden. Haughley parish records through the 1600s, 1700s and 1800s give extensive details of the relief of the poor and the system was perpetuated until the Poor Law Reform Act of 1834 eventually took the problem away from parishes. The workhouse was built at Onehouse and the records show that several Haughley people ended up in this unpopular institution, known colloquially as the 'spike'.

The Toy Fair

At some stage in the Middle Ages an annual toy fair was established and held on 15 August, the Feast of the Assumption, presumably because the full dedication of the church is the 'Church of the Assumption of the Blessed Virgin Mary'. A toy fair would have been rather like a street fair of today with various items for sale, as well as other amusements. The last recorded toy fair was in 1871. It was brought to a close because the fair had started to attract too many undesirable characters and had descended into something of an unruly annual party.

Other Housing in the Village

In the early-eighteenth century there was a fire that destroyed a number of cottages in Market Street, now Duke Street. The date is usually set as 1727, although there are some contradictory records. This explains why, opposite the church, there now stand light industrial buildings rather than the cottages that one would normally expect to see. However, inside the Old Mill there are still traces of the original cottage walls.

It must have taken some while for the rebuilding to commence because the current Old Mill building dates from about 1820, when a sash-cord mill was built opposite the church. In the church are the leather fire buckets that were held as part of the local fire-fighting equipment. The villagers would form a chain from the moat to the scene of the fire and pass buckets of water down the line.

Until relatively recently there was also a special long-handled rake in the church, which was used to pull the burning thatch off cottages so that only the roof was destroyed and not the whole house, which would have been largely timber-framed. The cost of the damage in the 1727 fire was put at £825.

In other places in the village some older houses survive. The Bell family established Old Bells and New Bells Farms just outside the main part of the village. In 1450 it was recorded that New Bells Farmhouse was rebuilt from the proceeds of smuggling wool out and silk into the country. On the road up to the A14 is Waterrun Cottage. This was formerly Fishponds Cottage and may well have been tied to the keeper of the fishponds when both the ponds and the cottage were the property of the Abbot of Hailes. There is a beam in the cottage into which are carved the arms of the Abbey of Bury St Edmunds. Many of the cottages in Old Street, although extensively rebuilt, have their origins in the Middle Ages. Dial Farm still retains some traces of ancient pargetting and the wooden porch is reputed to have come from Mary Tudor's estate at Westhorpe.

In more recent years Mid-Suffolk District Council, formerly Gipping Council, provided a number of council-houses and the village was extended considerably. Much of the credit for the improvements in modern sanitation and water supply go to a previous vicar, Revd Grainge White, after whom parts of the village are named.

A view up Old Street in 1920, showing sewage and foul water running down the gutters on either side of the road.

Chapter Two
Dwellings and Domestic Life
Sue Moore

What is immediately striking about images of late-nineteenth-century Haughley and the village around 90 years later, as depicted in the 'Haughley Photographic Collection' of 1989, is how little the village has apparently changed. There are the ancient street patterns, the straggling village green, the church, Revd Crawford's Coal House, the school, but, above all, the dwellings. A nineteenth-century time traveller would, even a further 16 years on from 1989, observe a very familiar low-level roofline, and a recognisable vista of colour-washed cottages. This is the historic heart of Haughley, the conservation area. What the time traveller would not recognise are the 'avenues', 'closes', 'ways' and 'views' around which new groups of houses have gradually developed, not in the main village alone, but out at Haughley Green and any spot in between that can support a few new dwellings.

For centuries the occupants of many of the pastel cottages looked to the surrounding farms and agricultural land for employment and sustenance. The census records of 1881, 1891 and 1901 consistently list the residents of Haughley, Haughley Green and Haughley New Street as being largely farm labourers, born either in Haughley or not much further afield than the encircling parishes. Male workers were sometimes more specifically noted as being a rakemaker, blacksmith, miller, shepherd, stockman, woodsman or thatcher. Then, from the mid-nineteenth century, other popular male occupations included platelayer and various jobs connected with the newly arrived railway.

As for female workers, most women had quite enough to do in bringing up their families. Something in the air out towards Haughley Green seemed to encourage the occurrence of larger families than the rest of the parish, at least according to the census listings. Neighbours in Green Road in 1901 were Harry and Jane Cooper, a farm labourer and his wife with five sons and three daughters ranging from two to 18 years, and William Williams, farmer, whose 40-year-old wife Alice had borne him four daughters and three sons covering the same age range.

Actually residing in Haughley Green at the same date were Charles Ager, stockman, and wife Kate with six sons and two daughters between the ages of two months and 15 years. Another Haughley Green family were James Moss, platelayer, and wife Mary Ann, both well into their middle age, who had living with them five sons and two daughters from three to 30 years, plus 11-month-old granddaughter Kate Cuthbert. In Duke Street Mrs Keeble, widowed around the time of the First World War at the age of 32, was left to struggle bringing up eight children single-handed.

Those women who did have paid employment are recorded as charwomen, laundresses or domestic servants, although there were some female innkeepers, such as Agnes Wallace (1901) and Ada Woods (née Dorling) who both offered hospitality at the Fox in Haughley Green, the latter during the 1920s, and Miss Mary Ann Brown, landlady of the Railway Inn in around 1879.

The Haughley Village Appraisal 2000 reveals that 25 per cent of the parish properties were built before 1900. These buildings that now lend so much charm and character to our ancient village were once mostly rented out to the kinds of poor working families described above. Quaint properties, that nowadays may be in demand for holiday letting, were once the last bastion against bitter Suffolk winters for families whose privations and labours sustained the tenuous rural economies of communities like Haughley.

Nineteenth-century directories such as *White's* and *Kelly's* continually repeated the potted, and sometimes inaccurate, histories of Suffolk villages, and followed them with a list of landowners, tradespeople and shopkeepers. Of course that was the express purpose of these directories, but they left unacknowledged the solid core of labourers' families. The ancient family names occurred sporadically – Denny, Faiers, Gladwell, Green, Hunniball, Jeffrey, Pollard, Pryke, Sore, and so on – and these names are still alive in Haughley in the early-twenty-first century.

The contrast between some of their lives and those of the so-called great and good was often harsh by modern standards. As noted earlier, it was not unknown for families of eight and more to be crammed into a total of four living and sleeping

Girls feeding the swans at the moat, c.1910. (PICTURE TAKEN FROM A SMITH'S POSTCARD)

Haughley School in 1901. Left to right, back row: H. Cornish (headmaster), H. Cutting, J. Cooper, F. Fenton, E. Ager, W. Murton, O. Jeffries, ?, M. Cornish (teacher); middle row: H. Clements, R. Dodson, W. Scott, J. Morphew, S. Green, W. Hart, S. Dodson, F. James; front row: O. Miles, E. Gladwell, N. Ager, J. Denny, C. Denny, A. Ager, N. Cutting, R. Taylor, C. Taylor.

Left: *Swans on the castle moat, c.1910.*

Below: *The King's Arms and Glebe House, c.1900.*

DWELLINGS AND DOMESTIC LIFE

Haughley Crawford's VC Primary School, 1910.

Mr N. Marsh and the pupils of Haughley School.

One of the classes at Haughley School in the 1970s.

❖ DWELLINGS AND DOMESTIC LIFE ❖

Kate and Harry Pryke with their children Horace and Hilda, c.1920.

areas. In parts of the parish some lived more comfortably and could afford to pay others to perform domestic duties for them. For instance, at Haughley Park Arthur and Mary Pretyman and their family occupied the house from the late-nineteenth century to the early-twentieth, with at least seven live-in servants to cater to their needs. Plashwood, too, had its governess, cook, house-, parlour- and kitchen maids in the late-nineteenth century. Not for these incomers the worry of fetching water from the pump, or the indignity of the night soil cart passing close by their parlour. But at least they provided some employment for local people. Despite their hardships their vigour persisted and has made Haughley what it is today.

It would seem fitting at this point to try to uncover what daily life was like in Haughley through the memories and experiences of local people. That 25 per cent of pre-1900 properties that remain are often just façades of prettiness, only outwardly reminding the modern observer of what once went on within. Interiors may have been sympathetically restored or coolly modernised. But no one now lives quite as they once did in these historic buildings, even during the hard days leading up to the Second World War. John Glyde, in his 1856 book, *Suffolk in the Nineteenth Century*, described the physical condition of the labourers' accommodation. Cottages before 1856, he wrote, were 'mostly clay-walled and thatched; they are warmest in winter and coolest in summer.' Those being erected by landlords from 1856 onwards were, he said, 'small, one brick thick generally, and pantiled. Others are built with large clay lumps.' He continued, 'Taking the county as a whole, the clay and plaster walls and straw-thatched cottages predominate.' Gerald 'Jed' Cooper, a local builder, described how these 'clay lumps' were made from 'clay with straw in it, cut into blocks, stamped down – all the straw is stamped down into it.' Then, while they were still 'green', they were 'cut into blocks, laid and 'faced up' just like you would with modern brickwork.' The excavation of clay on the building site left a large water-tight hollow which would act as a reservoir for rainwater. 'So', says Jed, 'that's how you got a little pond with almost every house!'

In Haughley such cottages might have been bought or constructed by a local family that had acquired a little capital and wanted an investment for old age and infirmity. The Woods and Palmers rented out small cottages to labourers' families, not so much for the rental income as for what a property might be worth at the death of the owner. In 1910 the entire row of cottages next to Cock Corner, in what was then Stowmarket Road but is now Fishponds Way, was sold for £350. By 1932 a single dwelling in that same row cost £171.10s. (£171.50). It was rural thrift and a way of providing a pension for a widow and her dependents.

In the smaller cottages there were few rooms. Downstairs there would have been a parlour and a kitchen, with no front entrance hall but maybe a back lobby. Rough walls with exposed beams were whitewashed, and floors of beaten earth or brick were covered with oilcloth or linoleum. In the main living area there might be an open fire or a small range. Thin lath and plaster walls, together with the phenomenon of 'flying freehold', by which adjoining properties might overlap, meant that any noise from your neighbours was easily heard. Doors and

Mrs Green emptying the household slops into the gutter in Old Street, 1920.

Above: *The wedding of Herbert Hart and Edith Florence Dorling, 1911, taken at Cobb's Place, Haughley Green.*

Right: *Mrs Keeble's back yard in Duke Street in 1920. All the household slops and sewage were disposed of within the yard.*

Below: *Beatrice White and Dennis Spink with the first pail of water following the installation of the water tank in Station Road, 1932. The tank fed stand-pipes around the village – before this all water was drawn using pumps or wells.*

Below right: *Walter Greengrass and Alfred James in the early-twentieth century.*

windows were ill fitting, so needed heavy curtains to exclude draughts. These cottages were small and plain, but comfortable enough. Dennis Spink recalls how he and his twin brother Harold, older brothers Lennie and Donald, and sister Enid slept head to toe, as they shared the two bedrooms of their cottage by the Folly with parents William and Christine. Speaking of his childhood in the 1920s and '30s, he described his mother's pride in her 'best room', which was 'kept aside and used on special occasions, like Christmas time or if any special visitors came.' So living in cramped quarters did not mean a lowering of standards of hospitality or respectability.

Enid Thompson recalls her mother, Edna Turner, taking the whole day on Mondays, in the mid-1930s, to do the family wash: 'She had no means of washing – my dad had to build a copper in later times. But to start off, well she used to boil her clothes on a Primus stove in a tin bath.' The copper may have had its water heated, as in the Dorling home in Spikes Lane, with wood embers from a brick oven. Sheila Marschalek's grandfather, Arthur Dorling, stockpiled a store of faggots made of hazel twigs and small branches, bundled and bound together with green hazel, to provide fuel throughout the cold weather. When hot water was needed for washing or bathing, glowing embers were placed under the copper filled with soft water that had been collected in tanks and tubs. On bath nights, tin baths that had hung outside all week were brought in and filled with hot water. The little ones got first go, with father being the last to take a dip. In between the water was often not changed, merely warmed up by the addition of more

The occupants of the cottages next to the forge on Old Street (now Bell Cottage).

water from the copper. This was a common practice and largely continued until council-housing with piped water arrived in the village in the 1930s.

In the heart of the village, water for this weekly event was drawn from the pump on the village green. Jean Brand revealed that, in 1944, 60 per cent of village people still used the pump, although Maurice Hart recalled some properties having a standpipe. Even in those years, well into the twentieth century, there was little or no running water as we would know it in 2005. The only sophistication might have been the ability to pump water through from the copper in the kitchen to the tin bath in front of the fire. Jed Cooper has seen farmhouses with pipes running diagonally across ceilings, taking the shortest distance in order to keep down plumbing costs. Appearances seemed not to matter

A domestic science class in 1940. The picture includes: Phyllis Balkus (née Faiers) *(back row, far left) and* Ruby James *(back row, third from left).*

The Elmer family, c.1900. Left to right, back row: *Gwen, Kate, John, Minnie;* front row: *Grandmother and Walter.*

The Mothers' Union in the Vicarage garden, c.1936. The picture includes: *Revd and Mrs Grainge White with their twin daughters Beatrix and Beryl* (far left), *Mrs Keymer with Alan* (middle row, next to the twins), *Mrs Paddy* (middle row, fourth from right), *Mrs Ager* (middle row, fifth from right), *Mrs Ag King* (second from right), *Jane Whitehead* (kneeling front row, third from left), *Mrs Brunning* (kneeling front row, fourth from left).

DWELLINGS AND DOMESTIC LIFE

Above: *Harry Pryke's wedding at Preston in 1908.*

Right: *Sale particulars of the forge from 1950.*

Below: *Minnie Nunn and a colleague, believed to be at Haughley House.*

HAUGHLEY

Particulars and Conditions of Sale of a
FREEHOLD
DWELLING HOUSE
situated at
Old Street, Haughley
with Blacksmith's and Wheelwright's Shops
Outbuildings, Garden and Orchard
in all about
2 ROODS   18 POLES
WITH VACANT POSSESSION ON
COMPLETION OF THE PURCHASE
which

WOODWARD & WOODWARD

are instructed to Sell by Auction in the
Saleroom, Station Road, Stowmarket
on
THURSDAY, JAN. 5th, 1950
at 3 o'clock in the Afternoon in One Lot

Vendor's Solicitors:
Messrs. GUDGEONS PEECOCK & PRENTICE,
Butter Market, Stowmarket, (Tel. 1).

Newby - Printer - Stowmarket

when weighed against the convenience of piped water. Flush toilets were an exotic luxury for country folk, and everyone dreaded the scent of the night soil cart on a Friday evening, as it arrived to empty buckets from outdoor privies. Eventually more modern amenities were installed in Haughley, but in some outlying parts of the parish running water was not available until the 1960s. Ernest and Caroline Dorling, at Spikes Lane, contrived to provide their own piped supply only by the means of a petrol-driven pump that raised water from their own well in around 1956.

The late arrival of the water-supply was accompanied around Tothill by mains electricity. The centre of Haughley was electrified as early as 1938, and the 66,000-volt cable had to pass across the Dorling land, Ernest Dorling giving his permission to the Electricity Board. But he 'omitted' to ask for written confirmation that Spikes Farmhouse would also be electrified, and so it was bypassed! Thus, oil-lamps and candles continued to be the order of the day. Meanwhile, Dennis Spink remembers the generous provision, in the main village, of three lights and one socket for 12s.6d. (62½p). This made for some difficult choices for William and Christine. They had six rooms altogether. So Dennis's mother at last decided on:

... a light in the living-room, a light in the 'best room', and my mother had a light upstairs in her room – so that's the three lights gone. We still had to use candles in our bedroom.

So, clearly, did many others. Naturally 62½p was a big expense in those days, so electrification was a gradual process, only achieved by families making economies in other areas of domestic life.

Although there is now a conservation area in the village, and people are familiar with the concept of listed buildings, Haughley is not a museum. Housing was erected and adapted, sometimes over centuries, to fit the lives and needs of the occupants. In the past, if something needed changing, then it was changed without the permission of committees, and this happened until fairly recent times. Eric Noy, of seventeenth-century Red House Farm, observed of the continuing alterations to his home of 40 years, 'Well, it's part of its history – the way it's evolved to the needs of people. Why not? We've altered it since we've been here. We've exposed quite a bit of it.' All around the parish walls have been inserted, then removed; windows enlarged and reduced; cellars filled in then dug out again; tiles have replaced thatch, and the converse. Jed Cooper, of Fishponds Way, has reminisced on his life as a local builder of 50 years who was called on to repair, renovate and even demolish some of these sorts of properties. After first working for Buck's of Stowmarket, he married Haughley girl Janet Cobbold, a descendant of the Sore family, and established his own business with Scotsman Jim Hutton in the late 1950s. Not only has he seen the concealed innards of many old buildings, both grand and humble, in the parish, but he also helped to build the new developments of Bixby Avenue (in 1954), Denny Avenue (1960s), and Ladyfield (1970s).

Haughley School in 1921. Left to right, back row: ?, ? Laurence, O. Rice, ? Lock, G. James; other rows include: L. Firman, ? Reynolds, F. Dodson, A. James, V. Gladwell, ? Mitchell, ? Baldry, T. Aldous, M. Talbot, ? Bloomfield, L. Elmer, Doris Diaper, G. Robinson, V. Green, M. Morphew, N. Arbon, ? Pleasance, T. Aldous, ? Bloomfield, ? Johnson (from Dagworth).

Haughley School in 1922. Left to right, back row: E. Pleasance, W. Thorpe, V. Peeling, B. Firman, Jack Murton; third row: N. Rice, B. Goss, N. Adcock, B. Denny, L. Avery, Francis Ayton, E. Armstrong, Dolly Andrews, S. Fellingham; second row: I. Bullett, May Cawston, G. Hart, K. James, ? Cox, E. Dorling, M. Hunnibell, E. Sore, Nora Wade; front row includes: T. Arbon, A. Aldous, B. Andrews, ? Andrews, V. Hart, L. Fellingham, Dick Arbon, Tom Stiff, Philip James.

Jack and Leonard Elmer with Aunt Gertie, c.1904.

An elderly lady, believed to have been a member of the Elmer family.

The Mothers' Union in the Vicarage garden, 1936. The picture includes: *Mrs Whitehead* (with tray), *Mrs Keeble* (seated front left), *Mrs Grainge White* (standing centre rear), *Mrs Lawrence* (seated front centre with daughter), *Mrs Pike* (seated on right), *Mrs Keymer* (standing with pram) *and Alan Keymer* (in pram!).

In spite of what we now may call disadvantages, so many of Haughley's present-day residents recalled happy, fun-filled childhoods when they came to the Village Hall on the 5 and 6 June 2004, to reminisce and commemorate the 60th anniversary of the D-Day landings. Of course, many of them were perhaps too young to have appreciated the sacrifices their parents made to create that stress-free domestic atmosphere. Eric Noy, now of Red House Farm, but whose wartime home was in Gipping, considered himself:

> *... quite lucky in my childhood in so much as I was two years old when the war started and I didn't know the relatively affluent times before the war. I was used to rationing, and I was used to wartime conditions, because I didn't know anything else.*

Sheila Dorling, around ten years earlier, remembers her mother Caroline's baking sessions. Although she apparently never made her own bread, her fruit tarts and pies were popular and, as Sheila herself admits, 'I was a fat child – having been the only one I suppose I got better sustenance than some did.' They always had roast beef, mutton or pork on Saturdays – never chicken, because that was a Christmas treat. On Sundays they ate the cold remains of the joint with fried vegetables and, if it had been 'a largish joint, there'd be some left and we used to have that with a suet pudding, gravy and vegetables. Tuesdays – might have had sausages, perhaps.' She also fondly recalls meat puddings, and 'fatty' liver baked with potatoes and onions. Sheila remembers that there was also:

> *... traditional pea soup, eaten for two or three hundred years, I should think, in Suffolk: dried peas soaked overnight and then cooked with carrot, potato, onion – meat if there was any about. This would take several hours to cook – very cheap, nourishing food for the peasants – which we were, of course!*

On top of this soup went suet dumplings topped off with butter. Sheila comments that ordinary people didn't worry about things like cholesterol in those days because they worked off the excess weight through sheer physical labour.

However hard life and work might have been for villagers there were still moments of leisure to be enjoyed. Sheila Marschalek's mother and grandfather introduced her early to the pleasures of reading, and she devoured classics by Defoë, E. Nesbitt,

Mrs Jeffries outside No. 1 Duke Street in the early 1900s.

❖ DWELLINGS AND DOMESTIC LIFE ❖

Above: *A class photograph at Haughley School in the 1880s.*

Right: *Kathleen Coe, Mrs Minnie Nunn, Mrs James and Johnny Nunn on the Folly.*

Below: *By the sea at Felixstowe on 25 July 1939. Left to right: ?, Fred Harper, Johnny Nunn, Mrs Harper, Elsie Harper.*

Above: *Hilda and Horace Pryke in the early 1900s.*

Left: *Mrs Davey in her garden at Old Hall Cottages, Haughley Green, c.1960.*

Contemplating the work that needs to be done in Mrs Keeble's garden, 1930s.

A family picture with Philip 'Sorta' James on the left.

The village pump and Old Street in 1946.

Mrs Fellingham at the corner of St Mary's Avenue.

DWELLINGS AND DOMESTIC LIFE

Richmal Crompton and Arthur Ransome. Dennis Spink, in the 1920s, was more of an outdoor fellow, and no doubt the games he played in his yard, then later in the unlit streets after he'd begun school, had been passed on by brothers and sisters for generations: marbles, spinning-tops and making pop-guns. He says:

Autumn time was when we used to make pop-guns – used to cut a piece of elder out the hedge – take the pith out and make a handle – and go and get a pocketful of acorns, and we used to amuse ourselves with our pop-guns. You tried to get the loudest bang!

Enid Thompson, in the 1940s, remembers congregating with boys and girls in Old Street, or cycling miles to neighbouring villages to visit friends. It may have been these same boys and girls that Billy Talbot, of Station Road, recalls 'hanging about' outside the fish and chip shop. Indoors, Donald Spink, Dennis's brother, listened to his crystal set, for there was no television and little radio in those days. In the 1940s teenager June Burman (now Makins) was a fan of the radio club 'The Ovaltinies', broadcast on Sunday evenings. Without cars, and no bus through the village for many years, families amused themselves close to home, regarding a rare day out in Felixstowe as a major outing. The Sunday school thrived in the 1930s, as Dennis Spink recalled: 'They used to organise a trip to Felixstowe. And... you'd get three double-deckers go out with children and mums. A big percentage of the village went.'

When foreign troops were stationed around Haughley during the Second World War, Gladys Morrison, then living in The Street, remembers doors being opened to strangers: 'In the family home we often had Polish or US airmen around, especially at Christmas. It was difficult with rationing, but cosy by fire- and oil-light.' Haughley's residents had to use their wit to banish the cares of the day, but they were not saints. Children were naughty, and parents at a loss for solutions, then as now. Bob King and Alan Keymer, in their early teens during the war, scoured

Jacky Keeble, Horry Pryke and Claude Pryke on a stile in 1932.

Doris Oram (née Baldry) with her mother outside the bungalow in Windgap Lane, 1937.

the countryside for bomb debris as souvenirs after air raids, incurring the wrath of the school's headmaster. The more visible presence of the policeman in village life may have helped keep a lid on potential youthful disruption. There was an occupied police house for many years, and Dennis Spink certainly recalls PC Allum's visits to the school to reprimand particular boys who had been up to no good.

Up until the Second World War there remained an atmosphere of self-sufficient deference that no doubt marked out rural communities from the industrialised sort. At any rate, Enid Thompson, her brother and parents, John and Edna Turner, were taken aback by the insularity of Haughley compared to the Derbyshire mining village they left in the 1930s. Speaking of the December night in 1936 when they arrived from the station she recalled, 'It was pouring with rain – no street lights, which we'd had at Homewood in Derbyshire. My mum thought she'd come to the ends of the world.' The Suffolk accent seemed impenetrable to her, as did the closely woven family connections of the people amongst whom they found themselves. Yet, when her parents began their newsagent business, Enid's mother found it strange that she could go around the village and windows would be open, doors wouldn't be locked. 'She used to open the door and put the papers in, and this was six o'clock in the morning.' So this rural insularity had nevertheless created a safe haven for families who, on the whole, trusted each other and feared no trespass or violence from their own kind.

The event that seemed to have the greatest effect on traditional family life in Haughley was the Second World War. It ruptured the insularity by sending men far from their homes. When they returned, heads full of different ways of doing things, they came back to a village where strangers had sampled the rural hospitality; where wives had taken on new and onerous employment, making bomb trolleys or welding rods; where children had come to understand the frailty of outdated customs. There were new jobs to be had; new music to listen to; different expectations of what was acceptable and, perhaps, a

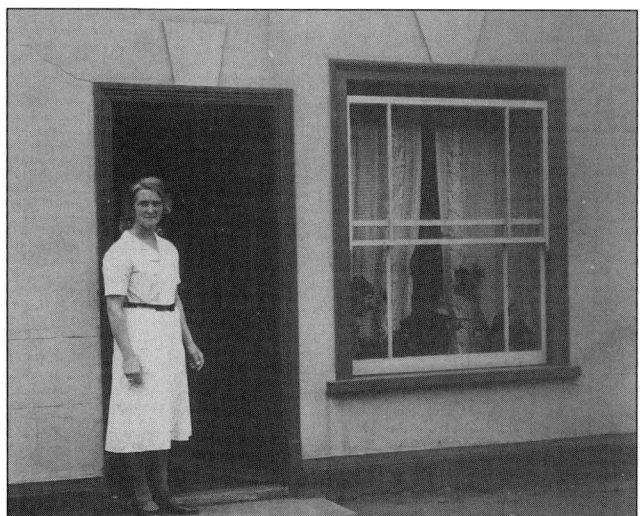

Mrs Minnie Nunn at the door of her house in Duke Street in the 1930s.

new restlessness. Ordinary people wanted things they had never had before, like warm, sanitary housing. Social housing had first come to Haughley between the wars, but after the Second World War it took off in earnest. These days most of us aspire to own our own homes, but it was the cheap-to-rent, solid housing in St Mary's Avenue and Station Road in the 1920s and '30s that gave villagers the first real hope of healthy futures and the chance to escape the tyranny of tied cottages and candlelight. In those early years, however, you still needed to remember your place in the village hierarchy. Dennis Spink recalls that the Church was influential in family matters in a way we cannot comprehend nowadays. He recalled that in the 1920s and '30s:

> ... you took it for granted that you should go to Church because if somebody who employed you on the land looked round to see you weren't in the Church... so you went to keep your job. When they built those houses up St Mary's and Station Road – all those white brick houses were built by Grainge White [the vicar was a member of Gipping Council], and because people wanted to move from an oldish house to a new house, they used to go to the Church to see the parson to put a good word in for them. The parson had a lot of sway in Haughley.

After the Second World War, when council-house building resumed, there were different criteria for getting onto the housing list. Many couples would spend 18 months to two years sharing with parents before qualifying, and the imminent arrival of a baby would not have harmed their chances. One of these postwar developments in Haughley was the Unity Housing Scheme, which created Bixby Avenue. Jed Cooper, working for Buck's of Stowmarket, was involved with this in 1954. The construction method used was based on a Scandinavian idea of the late 1940s, whereby concrete stanchions and 4x4 girders were bolted together on level footings to form a

Bony Davey in his garden striking a typical 'Old Bill' pose, c.1933.

skeleton. Jed remarks that this assembly of uprights was not dissimilar to fifteenth- and sixteenth-century methods of constructing oak-framed buildings. In Bixby Avenue the roof trusses eventually locked these uprights in position, at which point Buck's carpenters fitted 2-inch-thick concrete cladding slabs into the framework. On went the roofs and all the interior work could then be carried out in dry conditions. At a time when new social housing was in demand this method ensured rapid construction, and also attracted government grants for the local council. This kind of housing did have problems with damp in some parts of the country. But Jed insists that here in Haughley, because the work was carried out by skilled tradesmen, there were no setbacks. Their main drawback was in their unattractive appearance, which has been remedied in some cases by the addition of a brick skin. And the houses still stand in 2005, some 50 years later.

Two years after new family homes were built in Bixby Avenue, Enid Turner, now married to Derek Thompson, was raising her own family in nearby Windgap Lane. Postwar Britain was refocusing on home and family, so fewer married women were going out to work. Haughley was no different. Enid and other young village mothers used to:

DWELLINGS AND DOMESTIC LIFE

Mrs Alice Parker and John 'Tinker' outside their caravan in 1964.

Occupants of a new council-house in 1950.

Mr and Mrs Alec Faiers.

'Tinker' Parker (left) and Leslie Judd in the 1970s.

Jenty Parker, c.1964.

Above: *A 1950s view looking up Old Street.*

Above right: *Haughley School staff in 1963. Left to right: Leeta Chenery, Nora Mulley, Nesta Taylor, Norrie Marsh (headmaster) and Vanessa Shearing.*

Right: *Charles and Maud Fellingham and their daughter Jessie rest on the front fence at Fox Cottages, Haughley Green.*

Below: *Haughley School staff in 1957. Left to right: Mrs Allen, Nesta Taylor, Nora Mulley, Roy Holroyd (headmaster) and Leeta Chenery.*

Below: *John 'Tinker' Parker and his mother, Mrs Alice Parker, at their caravan door in the 1990s.*

DWELLINGS AND DOMESTIC LIFE

... get together and walk to Stowmarket, or go on the bus. We used to have a day at the swimming-pool, or meet, have coffee, and the children used to get together and play. My husband came home one night and there were 22 children on the front lawn – they were playing mannequin parades [1950s parlance for catwalk modelling!].

Haughley has doubled its population since the beginning of the twentieth century from 789 to over 1,500 at the time of the village appraisal in 2000. It is a popular and attractive area in which to bring up a family, and people still want to settle here if the continued building of new homes is anything to go by. In the village appraisal it was recorded that:

... part of the reason for Haughley's success... is that it is a well-balanced community. It is not a retirement village with only older people and holiday cottages; nor is it just a village full of young commuters or executives who have moved here because of the good road network. Haughley has a mixture of people, some of whom have lived here for all or most of their lives, and others who have come here because of the availability of housing, employment or because they know it as a friendly place.

It is also noted that, because of a 'diversity of house types', Haughley residents can move within the village 'as the size of their family changes'. In earlier generations people stayed put because they had few choices. These days, it would seem, they stay because it suits modern families. Perhaps Haughley is luckier than most rural communities in that it retains a Post Office, its school and one or two thriving retail outlets. The village has managed to adapt and absorb modern influences, yet still presents a picture of vibrant rustic charm to the outside world.

Sources
A. Booth, G. Clarke, K. Palmer et al, 1989, *The Haughley Photographic Collection*, Ancient House Press, Ipswich.
John Glyde, 1856, *Suffolk in the Nineteenth Century*, Simpkin, Marshall & Co.
Haughley 2000, *Haughley Village Appraisal*, Haughley PC/Suffolk Acre.
Nigel J.H. MacCulloch, 1983, *Haughley Past and Present*, Brokenborough Publications Ltd.

Suffolk Record Office:
Census records for 1881, 1891, 1901;
White's Gazetteer & Directory for 1855 and 1874;
Kelly's Post Office Directories for 1879, 1904, 1912 and 1929.

Unpublished:
Transcripts of tape recorded interviews by Sue E. Moore with:

Gerald Cooper	2004
Sheila Marschalek (née Dorling)	2004
Eric Noy	2004
Dennis Spink	2003
Enid Thompson (née Turner)	2001

Various reminiscences gathered at the Old Street Chapel on 17 January 2004, for the D-Day exhibition.

Margaret Cobbold with Tim and Karen Hart try out their bicycles outside the 'Unity' houses in Bixby Avenue in 1970.

Above: *A view from Cock Corner up Station Road to the Post Mill, c.1920. It is said that the mill was erected with the help of soldiers in 1815 and was burnt down in 1943, shortly before it was planned to be put back into use as part of the war effort. A cigarette end may have been the cause of the fire!*

Left: *A business card from Burgess Crisp Factory.*

Looking down from the village green in the mid-1930s.

Chapter Three

Haughley at Work

Colin Hart

It is Monday morning and Haughley is starting to stir. The sun catches the east side of the church tower, the rooks leave the trees on the Castle Mound for a day's foraging. The clock strikes – it is some time between the First World War and the still unforeseen Second World War. Let us take a walk around and see what the people of Haughley are up to.

We are standing at Cock Corner and up on the top of the hill the sails of Sam Goode's post mill turn, grinding some of the wheat from Hill Farm no doubt.

At the old Cock Inn Mr Harbutt has planted some fruit trees, which he brought with him when he recently moved from Red House Farm. He has got more space here than he needs, and will shortly be letting off half of the property to young Maurice Hart from Haughley Green – an incomer!

Further up the street past the cottages of 'Tinhat' Cutting, 'Khaki' Taylor, 'Hooter' Reynolds and 'Monkey' Moyes, lives William Rice, the chauffeur for Haughley House. He is waiting for the Coach House in the Folly to be converted into living accommodation. Next door lives Mrs Tipple, the District Nurse who travels around on her bicycle.

Near to the end of the row we come to our first shop – a sweet shop owned and run by Mrs Rosa Butterworth. Nearby we can see the severe figure of Wallace Allum, the village policeman. Rumour has it that he keeps a ball bearing in the finger of his black leather glove. Many a youth has felt that when dealt a 'smack across the skull'.

Now set back a little and under the shade of a huge walnut tree are the premises of Ernest Denny and his son Rowland, village butchers. They have just slaughtered a bullock that has been fattened up on the meadow behind. We can tell that by the blood-tinged water running from the hole in the wall and thence down the edge of the street.

A sad day – the walnut tree comes down and the appearance of Old Street is changed for ever in 1931.

Wallace Allum has just met the parish clerk and they are looking up into the walnut tree – is something amiss?

Now to Walnut Tree Cottage where Edward John Pryke leaves in his pony and trap to visit his son's harness shop up the street, for some replacement harnesses. The Forge has already this morning shoed horses from Dial Farm and Castle Farm and Alec Faiers is expecting young Herbert Coe from Redlingfield to visit today, seeking a job as a blacksmith, training under Mr Heffer.

Next to the Forge Victor Plummer, wheelwright, carpenter and undertaker, has just completed a coffin for someone who died last week. Did you spot that young lady heading up the street? That was Nora, Victor's daughter who teaches at the school.

A little further on we come to one of the village shoemakers and repairers – Con James is in business with his son Philip who is known locally as 'Sorter'. Repairing shoes is big business these days as villagers walk to most destinations – only a few have cars.

Over on the green Johnny Nunn, one of the village coal merchants, takes out his second load of the day from the decorative red-brick coalhouse. His horse is due for shoeing tomorrow after he has collected coal from the station.

Between Con James and Rapper Row the houses are unoccupied and falling down. The rain soon washes away the clay daub when the thatch is in disrepair. The slops run down the street from Rapper Row. The names of the occupants of these small houses sound Haughley through and through – Noddy Wilding, Fred Bullett, Daniel Green, Stubb Arbon, Bun Hart and Uncle Tom...

Opposite and exuding smells of flour, yeast, dough and freshly baked bread are the premises of Palmer's, the village bakers and newsagents. Now the second generation baking here, the family live above the premises. William E.G. Palmer is head of the household and sons Ronnie, Tom and Roy are being encouraged to play their parts in the business. Aunt Maude is the main contact with customers in the Bake Office.

The Post Office is well and truly busy in the ownership of Mr Alfred Woods. The postmen are John Cawston, George Sore, William Edwards and Harry Pryke. They are off now on their rounds around the village, Haughley Green and Haughley New Street. Generally they walk in the morning and cycle in the afternoon.

Above: *The pump and the walnut tree in Old Street, 1907.*

Left: *The west end of Old Street, c.1930.*

Left: *Palmer's Bakery, the King's Arms and Rapper Row.*

Below: *Building work in the 1930s. The picture includes: Fred Brand (far left), Jack Brand (third from the left), and Philip Pask (fifth from the left).*

HAUGHLEY AT WORK

Above: *Palmer's deliveries, c.1920.*

Right: *The account from Victor Plummer for providing a coffin for Mr Jeffries, 21 March 1931.*

A summer view of the walnut tree and Old Street in the 1920s.

MISS K. A. JAMES,
DRESSMAKER,
PIANOFORTE LESSONS GIVEN,
THE FOLLY,
HAUGHLEY,
STOWMARKET.

Alfred Woods is a man of many parts and influence in the village and his daughter Mabel is now Mrs William E.G. Palmer.

Adjacent to the Post Office is 'Mashes', the main retail outlet in the village. Run by brother and sister Frank and Kate Mash, they sell just about everything – clothes, groceries, sweets and pork. They have just rendered some pork fat down to lard and no doubt some of the boys coming from school will wish to scrounge some of the pork scratchings before going home. These will be eaten with bread, butter and a little vinegar. The workers here are Sam Lee, Reggie Ruffles and Pip Sore.

Just out of sight we can hear the children at school, playing during their midday break. The boys will be digging the school garden and the girls will practise laundry work when they return to their studies. These are normal lessons for Monday – tomorrow it is woodwork for the boys.

Ricky Saunders is the school's head teacher and the staff include Nora Plummer, Elsie Harper, Miss Scotchmer and Miss Goode.

Walter Runneckles is the landlord of the King's Arms which is now a Greene King public house, it being formerly a Cobbold's establishment. This area is the centre of village life. We snatch a quick pint, while George Robinson enjoys a 'Creamax' ice-cream from a travelling salesman.

Turning into Duke Street we pass No. 6, the home of Polly Lucky the church organist, who this morning is giving a piano lesson to Kathleen James. Over at No. 1 Mrs Harry Bowers is taking in the laundry from the Bevans of Plashwood.

At No. 3 stands Mr Harry Pryke, village harness maker, taxi driver and barber. He has fitted the new bridle to his father's pony and is now waiting for Roy Palmer to come over for a haircut. Later he will drive his Morris with a dicky seat to collect a customer from Haughley Station.

Further up Duke Street the corn mill is busy converting barley into meal for Farmer Whitehead of Haugh Farm. Bob Adams, who succeeded his father Cornelius to this position, runs the mill. The workers at the mill are Frank Green and Charlie Morfew, who are proud of their new lorry.

Past the church we come to the Vicarage. Revd Walter Grainge White, now recovering from his busy day of the week, is turning his attention to sewage! He is campaigning to rid the village of its stinking gutters and introduce a modern drainage system. One of his main concerns is Mrs Keeble across the way; she has eight children and has to dispose of the contents of her privy in her very narrow garden. All her slops are thrown onto the 'cinder heap' at the end of the yard. Let us hope he will succeed. Meanwhile, his green cycle with basket awaits an afternoon journey out for tea and cakes with one of his parishioners.

Opposite the moat at No. 18 Charlie Pollard is making a pair of new boots for Mr Gent of Castle Farm.

Charles 'Bar We' James lives at the rakemaker's house and workshop. His place will soon be taken by Tom 'Lish' Cutting. The ash wood is cut in the winter, stood to dry and then made into rakes for hay making and scythe handles.

Next door at Klondike Villa is the sweet shop of Nat Hood. The Hood family were also involved in building and this property together with some others in the Folly are examples of 'Cocky' Hood's expertise in decorated brickwork. The core of Klondike Villa is ancient, perhaps an early cruck house?

Now into the Folly, past the rakemaker's wood-drying ground we come upon the boarded barn housing Palmer's horses Scott and Polly. Bert Aldous has just watered them both in the nearby moat. Bert is looking smart – we understand that he has just returned from asking Mrs Creagh if she will let him rent the house soon to be vacated by Chauffeur Rice in Old Street. Bert is hoping to be married soon and wishes to move from Haughley Green into the village. Later on he will be cutting hay.

William 'Titafalol' Francis works as a horseman at Dial Farm. When he grooms the horses, he saves the hair from the mane and tail, brings it home and makes brushes of all types and descriptions. Sometimes he incorporates a design or words with different coloured hair. His brushes last a long time and will still be in use many years hence.

Folly House is our next port of call, the home of Edgar 'Squity' Woods, brother of postmaster Alfred. The coach-building business is now in decline and things are on the move. Neighbour Tom Cutting will soon move to the rake factory and the Colbys will move from the Elms to make way for 'Bar We'.

The Post Office, c.1935.

HAUGHLEY AT WORK

Above: *John George at the controls of his traction engine at Wetherden Hall, 1921.*

Right: *Mr Ayton's builder's yard (now 60 Old Street). Left to right: Horry Pryke, Tom Green, Herbert 'Whacky' Edwards, Tom Ayton.*

George Robinson buying an ice-cream at the corner of Duke Street mid-1930s.

Above: *Travelling knife grinder, Walter Parker, pictured in 1942.*

Left: *Harry Pryke, harness maker, c.1900, holding up the door of his shop!*

Looking along Duke Street towards the Mill, 1932.

HAUGHLEY AT WORK

Above: *Harry Pryke standing at the door of his harness shop at the corner of Duke Street, 1911.*

Above right: *Harry Pryke's harness shop is no longer here in 2005, but Mary Shave keeps a seasonal window display for the enjoyment of passers-by.*

Middle right: *Marrable & Son Antiques business card. For several years the business was run from the disused mill building opposite the church.*

Right: *The west end of Duke Street in the 1920s – deserted, not even a duck!*

Below: *The Hood family pose outside Klondyke Villa, now Bosmere Cottage, at the west end of Duke Street. The small building attached to the house was later a sweet shop. (POSTCARD, GIBSON AND CO, GATESHEAD ON TYNE.)*

C. J. Marrable & Son Antiques

Telephone:
Haughley 8158 (9 a.m. - 5 p.m.)
Stowmarket 4584 (24 Hour)

V.A.T. No. 250-9427-62

The New Mill,
Duke Street,
Haughley,
Stowmarket,
Suffolk.

Major Creagh in his garden at Haughley House, 1936.

The King's Arms and Palmer's Bakery, 1993. (PHOTOGRAPH GEOFF CLARKE)

HAUGHLEY AT WORK

The Woods family, master coach makers, c.1890. Mabel, in the driving seat, later married into the Palmer family, thus bringing two of the longer established village families together.

The day is getting on into the afternoon and Mrs Billy Spink prepares tea for her son Dennis who is returning from school. After tea Dennis will fetch water, and then play with his hoop and stick in the Folly. His dad, William John, will return from working at Nobel Paints, Stowmarket, and after his evening meal will feed the pigs in the garden. It will then be dark!

Round now to the big house in the village, Haughley House, the home of Major and Mrs Creagh. This household provides significant employment for village folk – not only to William Rice the chauffeur, whom we met earlier, but also his wife who does the laundry, Cissy Pollard who is cook, Daisy Taylor the housemaid, Edith Simpson the chambermaid, and Alfred Edwards and Walter Haxell the gardeners. With the advent of labour-saving devices future households will have less people 'in service'.

Opposite, at the Village Hall, sages William 'Noddy' Wilden, 'Tip' Hunnibell and Robert Wilding have drifted back from watching cars on the high road and are going to read the 'Anglian' beside the fire in the Reading Room. They are all retired, the former two being railway platelayers and the latter a farm worker.

We are overtaken by a small herd of cows coming up from the low meadows for afternoon milking at Alec Faiers's Dial Farm. They graze on the village green as they pass, leaving well-worn tracks. When milking is done Mrs Faiers will serve milk to jugs and cans passed through a small opening in the farmhouse kitchen wall. She is so small that many of the younger customers cannot see her – the only contact is by word – 'Half a pint, Mrs Faiers please, for Mrs Pulford, it's her daughter here'!

Continuing down Old Street we peer though the shop window of Frank Barrett, village tailor. He follows in the footsteps of his father Alfred and is busy making a pair of tweed breeches for the young Mr Horace Pryke. 'Horry' is intending to wear the new garment when he next takes his new Ariel motorbike out with Walter Thorpe and Charlie Murton.

At Chilton House we meet the slight figure of Cyril Adams and his dog Wickham coming back from his smallholding in Station Road. There Cyril keeps some pigs, hens and rabbits, and he is carrying a basketful of brown eggs. Cyril is son of Bob whom we met at the mill. 'Home' boys have joined the Adams household – they are Harry Rutherford and Johnnie Clarke.

Just before the Congregational chapel we come to four cottages, soon to be converted to the row of buildings that we know in 2005. In the one nearest the chapel lives Herbert Brand. Herbert is the founder of H. Brand & Sons, builder, contractor and decorator, sign writer, grainer and glazier. All kinds of jobbing work done, the sign says! The sons in later years are Billy (bricklayer and organist), Freddy (carpenter), Jack (bricklayer), Albert 'Tubby' (bricklayer), Wally (plumber), Eric (bricklayer), and Ray (carpenter). One daughter completed the set.

We come to another small shop – Sanders, a barber's shop selling newspapers and sweets. The Don Stores is yet to come and in its place stand thatched medieval cottages like those opposite.

A more recent property in Woolpit white bricks belongs to Dick and Ann Clarke who are coal merchants. In part of the property live Mabel Ransome and her brother 'Bunto' – two eccentric characters rumoured to be connected to the Ransome empire in Ipswich.

Now at the bottom of Old Street again, we are visiting Bert Ayton, local builder and undertaker, with a good well-established reputation.

It is now getting into the late afternoon and Dr Hunter at The Firs has returned from his rounds for evening surgery. He travels through the parish and beyond on his trusty cycle with leather doctor's bag slung from the crossbar. He is now in the dispensary

Last of Haughley's summer wine – William 'Noddy' Wilden, 'Tip' Hunnibell and Robert Wilding.

and we can hear the bottles clinking together as he dispenses one to the other. Is it the stress of the day or does he need some attention himself?

One last visit now to Firs Farm, Fishponds Way – Walter Denny, dairy farmer and local stalwart. Does he know that one day a road will be named after him?

We turn at the end of the village, in a road with neatly clipped hedges and tennis-court opposite, and get a glimpse of the thatched cottages in the late-afternoon light, with smoke rising in the still air. Folk are returning home at the end of another working day.

Above: *Cooper's grocery shop, before a brick façade was built over the timber frame (now the Long House).*

Left: *Harry 'Waxam' Pryke, harness maker, and his assistant.*

Below left: *Cooper's grocery in Old Street before Mr Burgess's time. The brick face had been built over the original clay lump and this was subsequently rendered to return the appearance to something similar to the original. (It is now The Long House.)*

Below: *The view from Haughley House, looking across the Village Hall and the Old Mill towards the church.*

HAUGHLEY AT WORK

Above: *Old Street in the winter of 1904, with children gathering under the walnut tree. Note the open drainage for rain and household waste water.*

Right: *John Elmer's harness-maker's shop, Christmas 1906.*

Below: *The 'Don', predecessor to the Co-op, in 1949.*

Above: *The Brand family in 1927. Left to right, back row: Walter, Jack, Albert (Tubby); front row: William (Bill), May, Doris, Herbert, Eric, Fred. A further child, Ray, was born in 1928. Jack, Albert, Walter, Eric and Doris all served in the Second World War.*

Left: *A view of Cock Corner at the turn of the twentieth century, with the Cock Inn pub sign and a cottage standing where the bus shelter is in 2005.*

Below: *Old Street, showing the newspaper shop in 1936.* (Photo Bell's Photo Co. Ltd)

HAUGHLEY AT WORK

The Special Constables of Haughley. The back row includes, from left to right: *Tom Cutting, John Aldous, Charlie Brunning, Fred Harper* (fourth from right, back row), *Harry Pryke* (third from right, front row) *and PC Jackaman* (second from right, front row).

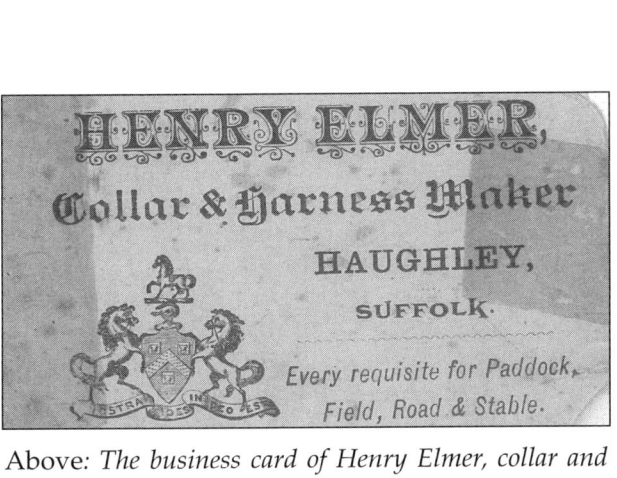

Above: *The business card of Henry Elmer, collar and harness maker.*

Right: *An early shot of the bottom of Old Street, c.1900, showing the site of the Co-op store in 2005.*

Munitions workers at Stowmarket in 1916. Caroline Eastall is in the back row on the far right.

Fred Harper (back row, third from left) as part of the MT unit, Army Service Corps at No. 2 base British Expeditionary Force, Rouen in 1915/16.

Chapter Four

Haughley at War

Howard Stephens

Haughley and the inhabitants of Haughley have seen their fair share of the turmoils of war. No doubt some of our local predecessors were involved in the struggles between the Iceni and the Romans, and recorded elsewhere in this book is the siege of the castle.

In the Middle Ages Haughley was required to provide seven soldiers and their corselets and muskets towards the standing army of Stow Hundred.

It is recorded that the First of Foot, the Royal Scots, passed through the village in 1688 on their way back to Scotland. Their commanding officer had been replaced by an appointee of William of Orange and they were ordered to embark for the Low Countries in support of William's interests. They saw no need to do this, mutinied and set off for Scotland.

It was troops on their way to embark for Marlborough's campaigns in the Low Countries and France that staged at Haughley and helped to build the windmill that stood in Station Road until the Second World War, when it was destroyed by fire in 1943.

The Napoleonic Wars were a considerable drain on the resources of Haughley. It had been decided that a militia should be raised to act as the home defence force against possible invasion by the French. This meant that as men were called up to join the militia, their families were left without support and so considerable sums had to be raised to help these families. It also meant that many who were selected to serve in the militia in fact paid someone else to take their place. To overcome this the government set up an Army Reserve for which service was compulsory if selected. The term of service was to be for five years and a bounty of £7.10s. was paid to the family. The parish records show a number of payments made to men selected for the militia and the Army Reserve, and even a year after the 1815 Battle of Waterloo, the parish was still paying out £24.10s.8d. to support members of the militia.

In 1782 Mr Ray, then the owner of Plashwood, made a generous donation towards the building of a gun-ship for the Royal Navy.

The First World War did not affect Haughley directly as much as the Second World War would do, but the loss of men was considerable and the war memorial bears testament to the many whose lives were sacrificed.

There were some attacks on Haughley; Mrs Aldous can still remember Zeppelins coming over the village with searchlights hanging below them. The vibrations from these vast airships made the church bells jangle. It was a Zeppelin that scored a direct hit on the Mid-Suffolk Light Railway between Haughley and Gipping on 2 September 1916.

During the Second World War Haughley lay in the middle of a cluster of airfields, the nearest being Great Ashfield, Rattlesden, Eye and Mendlesham. This made the area an attractive target for the Luftwaffe and, from the enemy's point of view, Haughley was relatively easy to find, for even on quite a dark night it was possible for an aircraft to follow the railway lines up to Haughley Junction and then peel off left or right to the target airfield. The distinctive pattern of the junction stood out well and the railway lines, conveniently for the enemy branched left toward Great Ashfield, straight on for Eye or up the 'Middy' for Mendlesham. It was not surprising therefore that many of the older residents have memories of the air raids.

Minnie Nunn in the munitions factory, 1916.

Munitions workers Louisa Hunnibell, Caroline Eastall, and May Clarke at Necol Munitions Works (later ICI), Stowmarket, in 1916.

Ted James (?), 1914.

Mrs Aldous and William Talbot both recall the doodlebugs flying up the street with flames trailing from the back. William's father was a road worker before the war and he was drafted into the Ministry of Works as a road 'ganger' during the war. One affect of the war was that it tended to make wages much fairer and it was only when he worked for the Ministry of Works that Mr Talbot senr started to be paid a decent wage. William had seen his brother called up for military service in 1941 and he himself was called up in 1945. He went to the Army Catering Corps and saw service in France, Palestine and Cyprus. He remembers the day the call came. He was asleep and his father and Sam Pryke came into his room with the call-up papers. In 24 hours he was at Stowmarket Station and on his way to basic training.

To try to counter the air raids there was a line of pillboxes with anti-aircraft guns, which stretched from Ipswich to Thetford and for quite a way the line followed the route of the A45 (now the A14). There were pillboxes at Harleston, Tot Hill and Squire's Cross and at Harleston there was also a searchlight post. In the village there was a roster of air-raid wardens, one of whom was established in one of the cottages that stood where the vet's stands at the time of writing. The ARP duty attracted a payment of six pence per day or night, Dial Farm provided a pint of milk, Palmer's Bakery offered a loaf or a cake and there was a pint from the pub, so the duty had its compensations.

Schoolchildren were also issued with gas masks in green tins and they were regularly put through the necessary training at school to learn how to use them effectively.

Several people, including Mr Hawes, remember firebombs landing in thatched cottages in Old Street one night. The fire was tackled by as many who could carry buckets from the pump at the end of the village green. Another firebomb landed in a corn stack on Mr Faiers's farm, where it remained apparently undiscovered and unexploded until the stack was thrashed. The bomb was fed into the machine where it exploded, but fortunately the machine was the only casualty. Many people recall seeing enemy aircraft passing over, presumably on their way to some other pre-designated target.

The railway junction saw quantities of munitions passing through on their way to the airfields. On one occasion the train coming down from the Norwich direction failed to stop, crashed through the level-crossing gates and damaged the signal-box. Bombs went rolling down the road but fortunately none of them were armed, so the incident ended without further damage, apart from a few cuts and grazes for those who dived for cover when they thought they might blow up.

Mr Hawes also recalls finding a small incendiary bomb, which he carried around for a while in his bicycle basket, until a neighbour suggested that it might not be a good idea! He took the advice and put it in a bucket of sand.

As the war went on prisoners of war started to appear and were often assigned to help with work on the farms. In the strange way of war some close friendships and relationships were made and some residents still receive postcards and letters from prisoners that they met during the war. Prisoners

The Post Mill, Station Road. Before the mill burnt down and when there were no houses in the immediate area, the mill was a highly visible landmark from miles around.

Fred Harper, Suffolk Regiment.

were based at Plashwood and the vicar, Revd Grainge White, occasionally invited some of them to the Vicarage for a meal. At Christmas things were inevitably a bit thin on the ground, especially once rationing was introduced, but many Haughley families hosted Polish or American servicemen over the Christmas period.

After the war, because of the shortage of labour many German and Italian prisoners were kept on to help with the farming. One such was Wilhelm Marschalek, who was eventually released at Christmas 1947. However, by then he had met his wife-to-be, Sheila, when he had been working in the fields, and he stayed on. In 1951 they were married in the church at Haughley.

If there was an air-raid alert babies would be tucked under the dining table – standard government advice. Mrs Aldous and others remember being strafed by a German fighter plane while walking across the fields, and it was quite normal to be challenged by a sentry if you wandered too close to any of the military accommodation or locations. Lewis Hart recalls a German fighter plane emptying its guns up the village street.

A recurring theme in talking to villagers about their wartime memories is that, in spite of the rationing, food was not a great problem. The choice might have been limited but everyone did their bit to produce what they could and there were plenty of chickens, eggs and vegetables. The older children would be taken out of school to help with the harvest or the pea picking.

Lewis Hart recalls that the flour tins from Palmer's Bakery were collected and painted dark green. They were then set up across the approach roads to the village so that they looked like mines from the air.

The United Reform Church lost its railings to the war effort and the metal was taken away to be recycled. Similarly, the iron railings around tombs in St Mary's churchyard were also sacrificed to the war effort.

A visit to the American camp was always popular, with access to cigarettes and sweets. William Talbot remembers seeing boxer Joe Louis on a morale-raising trip. Mrs Gladys Morrison remembers that her father served as a night watchman at the Great Ashfield airbase. He used to recount that the US B-57s went out by day and the UK bombers by night. Mrs Morrison herself worked on the railway, walking down the line and filling signal lamps.

Mrs Chapman worked for the NAAFI in Bury St Edmunds and met her husband over the NAAFI canteen counter in Gibraltar barracks. She also remembers doing her share of fire-watch duties.

In Old Street, where H. Brand & Sons ran their building business, the auxiliary fire pump was kept. Jack Ranson ran a local band that provided many of the local entertainments in the Village Hall and helped to raise money to send food parcels. He was assisted by Brenda Reed on piano, Jack Ranson on drums and Jack Keeble on guitar. Often it was Revd Grainge White who was the leading light in organising the dances and social events.

Dennis Spink in his Parachute Regiment uniform in 1944, prior to parachuting onto the Rhine.

Ernest Dorling in his Home Guard uniform in 1941.

Mr Burgess in his CD ARP uniform in 1943.

Sheila Marschalek recalls that in August 1944 a four-engined bomber, possibly a Lancaster or a Stirling, swept low behind the house and she could see the crew preparing for a crash landing. It ploughed into the ground near Dagworth and Sheila and her father were first on the scene. The aircraft had been ripped apart by tree stumps. One of the crew was killed and the others were badly injured.

The King's Arms was a popular venue for the Americans and the US Military Police would patrol the local streets to ensure that there was no trouble. Next to the King's Arms, at Glebe House, lived the headmaster of the school, Mr Rowles. He was also a member of the Home Guard. The Home Guard headquarters was at Palmer's office on the corner by the White House. One of their main tasks was to man the checkpoint on the A45 at Squire's Cross, where the activities and identities of those on the move were checked.

The playing-field was used for military training and there were troops stationed at Plashwood and at Haughley Park. In the run up to D-Day several logistic units, including Pioneer Corps and Royal Army Service Corps units, were based in the area. The trees along the avenue to Plashwood were cut back at a lower level so that the vehicles could be camouflaged and hidden from enemy aircraft. Subsequently, the Americans took over most of the accommodation.

Great Ashfield was the main base for most of the local Americans, although some support units were based at Haughley Park. The US records show that on 31 March 1944 581 Engineer Dump Truck Squadron, 923 Engineer Aviation Regiment, HQ and Service Company, 923 Engineer Aviation Regiment Medical Detachment and 2 Platoon, 980 Quartermaster Service Company, were all based at Haughley Park. Some residents remember US units based at Plashwood as well, but this may have simply been used as accommodation for the Great Ashfield airfield. The airfield was built during the First World War as an experimental base for the Royal Flying Corps, and it was not until June 1943 that it saw operational service, when 385th US Bomb Group and their B17s arrived. The servicemen from the base were billeted in many local villages.

The Commanding Officer was Colonel Elliott Vandevanter and the unit was nicknamed 'Vans Valiants'. The aircraft could be distinguished by its Group Identification Letter, which was 'G', painted in a large square font on the tail fin. Thus they were also called the 'Square Gs'.

On arrival in England they were allowed just three weeks' training before they were assigned to their first mission on 17 July 1943. The target was the Fokker factory based in Amsterdam. These were costly times for the Allied air forces and in the first nine days of operations the group lost four aircraft. A particularly black day was 28 July when one aircraft received a direct hit from a new air-to-air missile. The aircraft fell through the formation and took two others with it. A fourth was lost during the return journey. Losses at this rate were difficult to sustain and so the aircraft were modified for night flying. This involved cabin blackout and the fitting of flash and flame eliminators. The group flew its first night-time raid over Hanover on 27 September and one aircraft was lost in the raid.

The B17s were built as bombers but they had a formidable array of self-defence weapons on board. In a raid over Münster on 10 October they were intercepted by a large force of German fighters and the Americans shot down 34 enemy aircraft. Gradually the mission objectives moved eastward. On 4 March 1944 385th Group made its first sorties to Berlin and then, two days later, they led the 3rd US Air Division's attack on Berlin. The aircraft had just been fitted with a new ground-scanning system, which provided much better night-time navigation aid and the ability to undertake bombing raids 'blind'. However, Berlin was fiercely defended and the cost to the group was very heavy. A total of 15 aircraft were lost in April 1944, seven in one raid on Berlin on 29 April. But the unit bounced back and was awarded a second commendation, the Distinguished Unit Citation, for the effectiveness and accuracy of their bombing and their determination in pressing home the attacks. This was after some particularly successful sorties against German oil installations.

The avenue between the village and Plashwood, c.1930. The trees were trimmed back at a lower level to provide a convenient hiding place for troops forming up prior to the D-Day deployments in 1944.

US Air Force bomber crew at Great Ashfield in 1945.

US aircrew at Great Ashfield in 1944.

US aircrew at Great Ashfield in 1944. Steve Balkus is pictured on the right at the back.

There was a retaliatory raid by the Luftwaffe on 22 May when a single Junkers Ju88 bombed Great Ashfield airbase, hitting one of the hangars and destroying a B17 – the only B17 to be destroyed on the ground throughout the war.

In the run up to D-Day and throughout the Normandy landings the group was assigned to targets deep into Germany: Ludwigshafen, Berlin, Augsburg, Kassel and Chemnitz. As the Allied advance took hold the group deployed further and further away from Great Ashfield, with sorties to Stuttgart and Ulm. In general the losses started to lighten but on 1 March 1945 the group lost four aircraft in a determined Luftwaffe counter-attack.

A couple of weeks later and one of the group's aircraft was hit over Berlin but managed to fly eastwards, making a safe landing beyond the Russian front line – one of only 10 aircraft to escape eastwards during the war.

As soon as a ceasefire was declared the flying did not stop, but the payloads changed and the group was re-deployed to drop food for the Dutch during early May 1945. However, the war in Europe was over and in just a few weeks all the aircraft and aircrew had left Great Ashfield and the ground crews followed by the first week of July.

The group, which so many remember with great admiration and respect, was only based here for 22 months. In that time they flew 296 missions with a very high record of accuracy and success and they destroyed over 280 enemy fighter aircraft. The cost, however, was 169 aircraft lost and more 400 airmen killed. There is a memorial to the group and a Roll of Honour in All Saints' Church in Great Ashfield.

One of the wartime incidents that many recall is the dropping of number of bombs beyond Haughley Station. They failed to explode because they had been jettisoned, without being fused, from a B17 from Mendlesham, which had an engine fire on take-off and was forced to drop its bomb load and crash land. The relevant extracts from the group log are:

<u>Log of Aircraft Gallopin' Ghost/Queenie</u>
<u>August 15 1944 Assigned to 18th Squadron, 34th</u>
<u>Bomb Group, Mendlesham</u>

(Flew 36 operational missions between 17 Sep and 15 Jan 1945)

Mission 115 January 20 1945 Crashed at Haughley. B-17G 43-38332 B/Q Gallopin' Ghost with 18BS crashed on take off. Highest altitude reached was about 500 feet. 1 engine out with fire in the wing. Salvoed 'safetied' bombs in a field near Gipping Lane near Haughley. 4 men bailed out. Hulings chute did not open. Navigator missing. The other two were injured and are in hospital. The rest of the crew rode the plane in on the crash landing and are OK. Pilot: Mote. 2 killed in action. Plane salvaged. Four photos of crash are in Mission file.

Many of the men of Haughley went to war and, although the losses were nothing like those of the First World War, there were several who did not return and others who were taken as prisoners of war. It was inevitably a worrying time for all those left behind. Much was done to try to keep spirits up and ultimately to prepare to welcome home those who survived. The Village Hall was the venue for dances, concerts and social evenings and the Reading Room and games rooms were popular meeting places, although only men were allowed to use the

The catering team, preparing for a 'welcome home' fund-raising event in 1945. Left to right, back row: Connie Ager, Annie Pleasance, Mrs Keymer, Doris Reynolds; front row: Flo Ager, Harold Burgess, Lil Paddy, Mrs Firmin, Rose Green, Mr Bixby, ?, Mrs Spink.

Reading Room. Newspapers were provided free of charge. When a dance was organised the stage was erected over the billiard table.

On the ladies' side, the WI and Mothers' Union were both very active, supporting those whose husbands and sons had gone to war. Mrs Grainge White, the vicar's wife, is remembered well for all the effort she put into these activities.

Once the end of the war was in sight, the concerts and dances concentrated on raising money to give every returning serviceman a wallet and some cash. There was also a big 'welcome home' party.

The names of those who did not return, and of those who returned but did not recover from their wounds, are recorded on the war memorial and on a roll of honour mounted inside the church. The memorial was erected in 1920 and dedicated in March 1920. The original inscriptions were to the 28 men who were killed during the war. The memorial was rededicated after the Second World War but in 1947 it blew down in a violent storm and the top was broken off. It was eventually restored in 1995 and the names of the Second World War fallen were added, as well as the names of two whose deaths had not been previously recorded, but who died in service during the war.

In 2005 the memorial and the immediate area around it is cared for through the generous sponsorship of Mrs Maureen Edwards, in the Post Office, and much of the actual work has been completed by Dennis Frost.

The war memorial, pictured in 1920. The top came adrift in a storm in 1947. It was rebuilt and the top replaced in 1995. The figures at the top of the memorial are almost certainly identical to larger wooden carvings that once stood on the rood-screen between the chancel and the nave in the church.

A pilot of the US 385th Bomber Group and his B17 bomber at Great Ashfield in 1945.

Eva Bishop, later Mrs Tom Faiers, in her Land Army uniform, 1944.

Dedication of the war memorial in 1920. Note the iron railings around some of the tombs, which were taken away during the Second World War to be recycled.

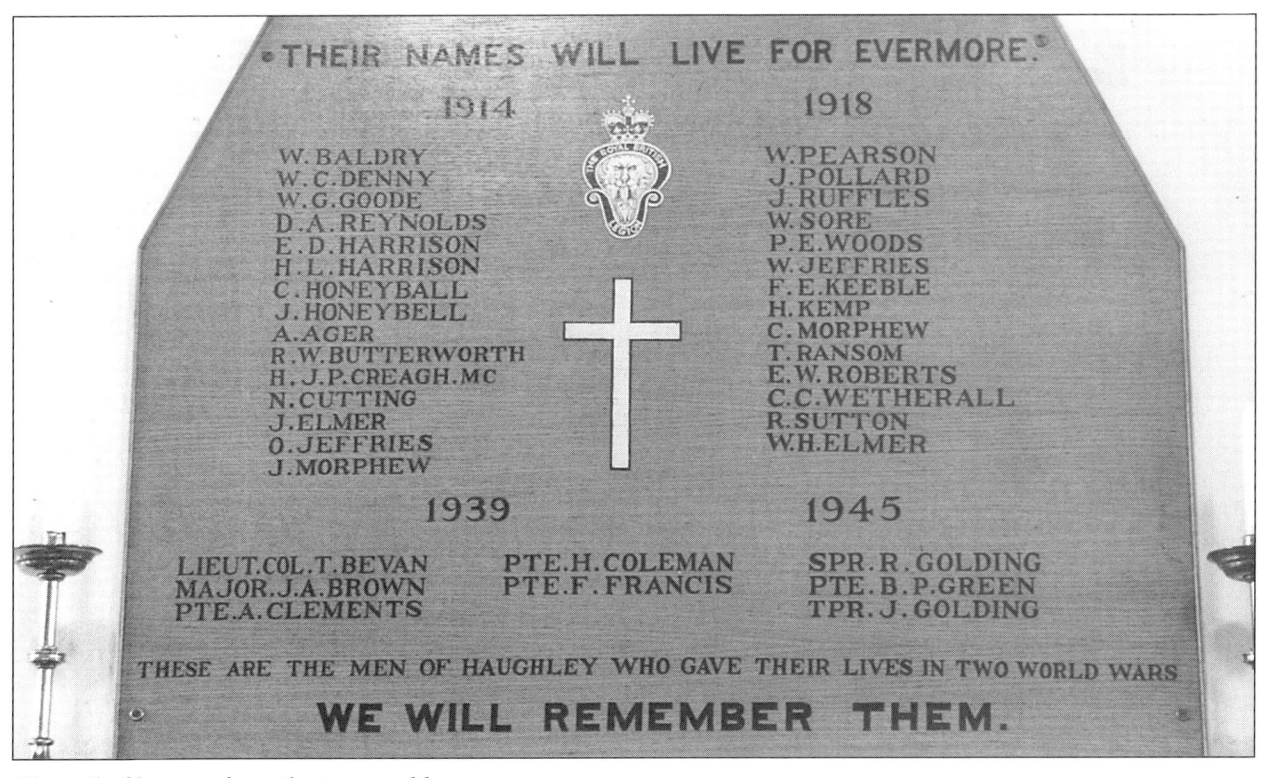

The roll of honour from the two world wars.

Above: *Flowers in the chancel for the 1979 flower festival.*

Left: *The church before the wall was rebuilt and pavements were provided in Duke Street. The open gutter used to carry away household waste water as well as rainwater.*

Below: *The flower festival in 1979 – an event held annually ever since – hit the local press. Pictured are, left to right: Pat Allum (later Eaton), Dot Arbon, Nancy van de Guht, Monica Prigg, Cheryl Forsdyke (née Allum), Mary Noy.*

Chapter Five

The Church of the Assumption of the Blessed Virgin Mary

Howard Stephens

The dedication is quite a mouthful and of course the name is normally shortened to St Mary or simply Haughley church, but the unusual full title is the first hint that there is more to our church than meets the eye.

We have to start way back before the Norman Conquest and try to fit the development of our church against the known pattern of church development in early England. In the second and third centuries churches as such did not exist, although some form of Christian religion was practised. The centre for this was an altar table, almost invariably made of stone, and perhaps some primitive shelter to keep the worst of the weather off the priest and those invited into the sanctuary. This was later to become the chancel of the church.

Not unnaturally, the congregations were not overjoyed at being left out in the cold and wet and so they started to build their own shelters and these eventually became the naves of the churches. This division of responsibility, the priest or patron of the church being responsible for the chancel and the parish for the nave, lasted right up to 1923! In fact even in 2005 the remnants of the system remain in that the diocese holds a small fund, called the Chancel Fund, which can be used at the discretion of the vicar, not the PCC, to help repair and maintain the chancel.

Going back to the fourth and fifth centuries, these early 'churches' were often placed at the highest point of the village – which is where they are today. Again, there are exceptions, but generally the church overlooks the village. This was also the natural place to build a lookout post for the village and towers were built from which a lookout or sentry could see the surrounding land and warn the village of the approach of marauders or other attackers. As early as the fifth century some of these towers had bells in them and these were sounded to call the villagers from the fields and back into the village in case of imminent danger.

These towers were called 'belfries'. This has nothing to do with the bells; that is just a linguistic coincidence. 'Belfry' comes from an ancient Flemish word 'belfroie' or 'belvoie' meaning a good view and therefore a place that affords protection. It is the same root as the word 'belvedere'. As some of these towers became more robust they also doubled up as the village strong room. There would be no stairs to the upper rooms, simply a ladder that was drawn up and, with simple wooden houses in the village, the tower offered the only secure place to deposit

Sketch of the church, c.1880, by Davy.

valuables and arms. The ringing chamber in many of today's early towers started life as the village armoury and treasury. At Mendlesham it is still possible to see the armoury with all its iron bolts and strong fortification.

Since both the church and the tower were competing for the high ground it was natural that they should eventually be linked into a single building. The use of the tower became more integrated with the church itself and the bells were used to summon parishioners to worship.

By about the eighth and ninth centuries churches as we might recognise them started to appear. Architecture and building techniques were primitive and the buildings were comparatively small and dark, but these were the churches that were in existence at the time of the Norman Conquest and this is the time when we can start to pick up the story of St Mary's with more certainty.

The Normans came from a strong religious background – many of the early orders of monks and friars were founded in Normandy – and the conquerors brought with them considerable Christian energy and zeal. The next 150 years saw an explosion in church building, the importation of stone from Normandy and the development of ever-improving building techniques. It is from this period that the vast majority of our earliest churches survive. They are characterised in particular by their narrow windows because the art of supporting a big window arch had not been mastered.

We know that there was a church in Haughley in 1080 and we can be reasonably confident that there was a church here for at least 100 years or so before that. However, the first definite proof is the record in the Domesday Book. By and large, churches don't

A view of the nave and chancel of St Mary's Church.

The top of one of the Perpendicular chancel windows, which obviously replaced an earlier window, with an infill at the top of the window.

move and the line that divides the chancel from the nave is almost invariably in exactly the same place today as from when the very first church was established on the site. But there are a few exceptions. Once built, churches tend to be rebuilt or extended where they stand, and so we can imagine that today's congregations sit or stand where the villagers of Haughley stood to pray 1,000 years ago. However, it is quite clear that the building has changed significantly.

This is a big building; in fact for a small village of 200 souls in Domesday, this is a massive church. Why? And if it was that big, why was it later necessary to extend the church by adding a south aisle?

Well, of course, the building we see in 2005 does not date back to Domesday. If we look at the windows, we can see that they are Perpendicular and point to the church being built in the period 1370–1440.

But if we look again at the windows, we have one odd one, close to the pulpit on the north side of the building. It is of a Decorated style from the period 1300–1370. The stone is old (where it has not been repaired) and is almost certainly the original stone. This gives us a good indication that this church was here in the 1300s and that the other windows were replaced at some stage in the fifteenth century. We shall almost certainly never know why this one window was not updated like the others – perhaps it was to commemorate a particular patron or perhaps it had recently been replaced when they decided to renew all the other windows. No matter, today it gives us a useful marker to the original date of the church. It is interesting to see that, in the chancel, the new windows did not quite fit the frames. On the outside this has been covered up with new flint work but inside you can see that there is a gap at the top of the windows that has been filled with rubble and mortar.

We have said that the church is big and it appears to be of a single architectural style. It is therefore reasonable to assume that it was probably built as a single project and funded by a wealthy patron. It does not take lot of research to find a likely candidate. We know that the honour of Haughley was granted to the wife of Edward II, Queen Isabella. She became lord of the manor and we know from the records that she spent some time at Haughley Castle, probably in a house located where Castle Farm now stands. The royal couple are known to have spent Christmas here in 1325 and their son Edward was christened here in 1326. The Queen would have brought personal wealth and a large entourage to the village and so we can see how and why such a church, much too big for the normal needs of Haughley, might have come to be built.

If we now look into the south aisle, we can see that the capitals, the heads of the columns that separate the aisle from the main church, are identical to those on the chancel arch. Capitals varied from builder to builder and from year to year. If there was a significant gap between two stages of building, then you can almost guarantee that the capitals will differ. Here they are the same and it is a safe assumption to say that the chancel arch and the arcade were therefore built during the same period, the south aisle perhaps being added during the building of the main church. The Decorated windows in the south aisle date from the period 1300–1370 and this ties in with the dates so far. However, it is reasonable to ask, if such a massive church was built in say 1320, why build an extension? Furthermore, the aisle does not seem to be of a sympathetic design to the light and airy feel of the remainder of the church. It is something of an anomaly.

To summarise where we have got to so far; we have a church rebuilt on the site of an earlier church. It appears to have been built as a single piece in about 1320, give or take a year or two, and at the same time or within a very few years it was extended by the addition of a south aisle.

It is time to move outside and to look at the tower. The first thing we can see is that it is not where a church tower is supposed to be. It is on the south side and doubles as the porch for the church. There are only 26 such 'south porch towers' in the whole of

THE CHURCH OF THE ASSUMPTION OF THE BLESSED VIRGIN MARY

The bell chamber openings with classic 'Y' tracery which dates to somewhere between 1200 and 1300.

England and of these 23 are in the Deben and Gipping valleys.

If we look at the tower we have our first surprise because, there in the porch and again high up in the bell openings, are 'Y' tracery windows. The stone in the porch windows is old and there is no reason to believe that these are not the originals. It was one thing to tinker with the wall of a church and replace one set of windows with another slightly larger set, but it was quite another thing to enlarge the windows in the tower; besides, there was no need because no extra light was needed in the tower.

This puts the date of the tower much earlier than the remainder of the church – some time in the period 1150–1300. We also know that church builders were very proud of their achievements and the best way to show off their work was to embellish the tower with decoration, possibly in flushwork – knapped flints placed in a pattern – and with their initials or emblem. Our tower is very plain, there is an almost total lack of decoration and so it was almost certainly built in the early part of the period, before the builders realised the advantage of advertising on their work. We shall be conservative and date the tower to 1200.

The next question is whether it was a freestanding tower or whether it was built as part of the church. The answer to this is provided by the buttresses. At the front they are diagonal, bracing around the corner of the tower, but at the rear they are square and always have been. They were designed to sit into the wall of the main building and we can be fairly certain, therefore, that the tower was built as part of a church. In spite of the enormous size of the church, there are no proper foundations. The strength of the walls and the tower relies solely on the thickness of the walls. A tower would only grow between 4 and 6 feet a year. Once that level had been reached, it was left to harden over winter and then in the next spring timbers were laid on top of the existing structure to provide the base from which the builders worked for the next few months. So that they could pull the timbers out once the stage was complete, builders set flat stones either side of the timbers and a bridging stone over the top, then laid the flints on this, leaving the timber free to slide out from its 'tunnel'. These holes for the timbers were known quite simply as 'put-logs' or, in Suffolk, 'puttlocks'. It was the puttlocks on our tower that led to the need for an expensive repair in 2001. The original holes in the wall acted as a line of perforations and the tower was quite literally splitting along the dotted line.

When we were looking at the inside of the church, we dated the south aisle to the Decorated period, about 1320, i.e., at least 120 years later than the tower, and so the question now is what was here before, or was the south aisle here from 1200? If you look at the string-course – the row of stone a few feet above ground level – it is very old stone and you can see that it is keyed into the wall all around the tower and along the wall of the south aisle. Furthermore, if you look closely in the corner where the tower meets the south aisle, you will find the stone is not simply butted up but has been cut to take the corner. That string-course has been there since 1200 and this dates the building of the south aisle to that same date.

The porch would have been open at the front and there would have been some wooden bars, which slotted into place to keep out cattle and other animals when the porch was not in use. Indeed you can still see the slots where these planks were set. The porch would have been used frequently as it was the business centre of the village. Legal transactions, major purchases, local laws and edicts would all have been dealt with here. It was, and remains to this day, the formal place for public notices to be displayed. The doors would have been added at some time in the 1500 or 1600s at the earliest. There is a date of 1677 inscribed over the door but this is unlikely to be genuine because if it had been written in 1677 it would almost certainly have been written in Roman numerals. Perhaps more convincingly, we have a photograph from the late 1800s and there is no date on the door!

Moving around the outside of the church, we can see that the south aisle windows are ornate and were obviously built to impress. It was quite normal for the public or open side of the church to be much more ornate than the other. There is a sanctus bell turret where the nave and chancel roofs meet. One of the assistants in the service would ring this bell when the sacrament was being raised and blessed so that the villagers who were working in the fields could stop and say a prayer.

There is also a priest's door in the south wall of the chancel and a well-defined path to it from the road.

As we move around to the north side of the church and look at the north wall, one thing is obvious – it is

Above: The tower and the south aisle, showing the string-course about a metre and half above the ground, which proves that these two parts of the building were constructed at the same time.

Left: The outer door into the tower, south porch. The door is a late addition, possibly from the seventeenth century. In medieval times the porch would have been open as it was the business centre of the parish. Simple bars would have been placed across the opening to keep animals out at night.

Below left: Detail from the west window of the nave showing the arms of East Anglia (St Edmundsbury) and Hailes Abbey, Gloucestershire.

Below: The clerestory.

THE CHURCH OF THE ASSUMPTION OF THE BLESSED VIRGIN MARY

a mess! The extension that houses the organ is clearly an addition, but there has been much other building and demolishing. There was actually a vestry here in early-Victorian times. It was pulled down and the organ was placed in a newly built extension some time later in the Victorian period. If you look very carefully to the left of the organ bay you can just pick out the outline of an older door – the entrance to the vestry from the chancel.

If you then stand back from the church and look at it from across the graveyard it is possible to see any major alterations that have taken place. Laying flints is like handwriting and you can tell where one team ends and another begins. What we want to see here is if there is any discernible difference between the chancel and the nave and then, looking at the nave, whether there is evidence of the roof being raised and a clerestory inserted. However, care must be taken in assessing buildings in this way, because modern restoration work can often give false clues. The flints confirm that nave and chancel were built as an entity, but it is easy to pick out the new work at the top of the nave wall, where the clerestory windows have been inserted. It is quite possible that, until the roof was raised to take more windows, the original roof ran in one line over both chancel and nave.

The other factor that stands out again is the total absence of any decoration. There are no niches, emblems, flushwork or stone carvings. It is simply a big, plain church, which is strange because we have already considered that it might have been built for or indeed by the royal family. Whilst we are behind the church it is also worth noting the stone buttresses. A few years ago a visiting expert dated the lichen and the stone to about 1200, possibly earlier.

Finally, from the west end of the church, above the main west window, you can see the complete change in flint work, out of character with anything we have noted so far. It is possible that this provides evidence of the clerestory having been added. It is more likely, especially given the rather coarse nature of the work, that this was done later, when the traditional flint-building skills were not as well honed as they had been in medieval days. Looking at the general arrangement of tower, aisle and nave it is quite clear that the tower was built to go with the south aisle and the nave is really part of a quite different building stage.

We have established with reasonable certainty that the tower and the south aisle were built at some time in the early 1200s. It is inconceivable that the main church, with its massive structure and vast spans, could have been built as early as that and so we have to change our whole outlook on the development of this church. It seems fairly certain that the original building was just the tower and the south aisle. It would have had a thatched, pitched roof and windows with 'Y' tracery all around.

It would be useful to have some collateral to support this theory, and indeed we have. If you visit Culpho or Ufford you will see two south porch tower churches of almost identical design and size as this tower and aisle. If you visit Brettenham, Akenham, Culpho or Nickfield you will see very similar churches, to which small aisles and/or a chancel have since been added. This particular team of builders, who gave the Deben and Gipping valleys all the south porch tower churches, worked to a single design.

It was only when the manor passed into royal hands, and it was necessary to provide a much larger church, that the north wall was removed and the new, much bigger church was added to the north of the original. The stone, of which there is a scarcity in Suffolk, was salvaged and the old stone used in the building of the buttresses of the new north wall.

Imagine, this small church where the south aisle now stands. There would have been no seats and so there was room for the entire village to squeeze in. The altar would have been in the same place as the current altar table and there was a piscina and sedilia for those officiating at the service. This area would have been screened off as a small sanctuary and it is

The north side of the church, showing the variety of windows and flint work.

Right: *The west end of the church.*

The Church of the Assumption of the Blessed Virgin Mary. (Photograph Arthur Bugg, 1898)

The south aisle looking westward – was this perhaps the original church?

likely to have been quite ornately decorated. You can see from the height of the piscina and the sedilia that they are slightly too high to be practical – this is because, originally, the sanctuary would have been raised slightly, and it was probably flattened at the time of the Reformation.

After the new church was built, the roof was re-pitched as a lean-to and the original church became an aisle or chapel. In fact, there is a record of the Chapel of the Holy Cross at Haughley in manuscripts from the fifteenth century, and a record of 'an image of Mary' and a cross being in the chapel. It seems likely that this part of the building was used as a chapel for travellers, possibly on their way to pay homage at the tomb of St Edmunds in Bury St Edmunds.

The roof has some fine carved angels in matched pairs. They have recently been restored by Rob Lewis. These angels were probably added at some later stage, possibly even as late as the Victorian era, but probably a century earlier. However, if you look behind these angels, at the east end of the aisle you can see traces of some much older carvings. The carving only survives on the south wall – originally it would have gone all round the sanctuary, but when the roof was re-pitched the only wall that was left untouched was the south wall.

Now we can look at the main part of the church from a slightly different viewpoint. This is the new extension to what is now the south aisle. It was built, we have decided, in about 1300–40 and at some later stage, perhaps 70 to 100 years later, the windows were replaced by the current Perpendicular windows. At the same time, because it was the fashion and was probably deemed a good idea, the clerestory was added. There is further support for this in an early-sixteenth-century will which leaves money for the roof of the new north aisle. Like windows, wills are risky tools to use as evidence. The fact that there was a will is no proof that it was executed or that the funds were applied correctly. It seems, however, that because there was a will there was an intention to build a north aisle, and that was probably a further reason for adding the clerestory.

Let's just pick out a few items of interest, starting from the back of the church and working forward. The west window is a fine, big, light window. It may well have had more ornate glass originally, but now there are just a couple of traces – tiny coats of arms in the stained glass, way up at the top of the window and so small that it is almost impossible to work out what they are. They are in fact the arms of Hailes Abbey in Gloucestershire and the King of Anglia.

In medieval times, if there had been a choir (and it is quite likely that there was one, given the royal patronage), then it would have stood at the rear of the church, below the west window. This was a nice light spot to read the music and the words – if they had any!

In the arcade, although the columns are hexagonal, the bases are square, reflecting that the bases are remnants of the former wall and the pillars have been built on top of these.

Looking back to the rear and north side we see the vestry door. It does not take much to see that this door was not built into the original wall with a well-formed arch, but has since been cut out in as regular a pattern as possible. This was done to add the vestry and subsequently a small coal store from when the church had coal-fired central heating! Work in 2005 to remove the dry rot in the floor in this corner has revealed a brick tunnel that was probably the conduit for heat from the external boiler house to the nave of the church. This is all part of the

The west façade of the church in the 1940s.

THE CHURCH OF THE ASSUMPTION OF THE BLESSED VIRGIN MARY

Above: *The south aisle looking eastward; the Decorated window has excellent Victorian stained glass.*

Left: *The magnificent East Anglian font in the church.*

The church clock, donated by the Bevan family of Plashwood in 1903.

Above: *A view of the arcade between the chancel and the south aisle, June 2005. Note how the chancel arch to the left appears to be identical to the arcade arches.*

Right: *The piscina and sedilia in the south aisle, both of which are a fraction too high for comfort. This suggests that they may have once been in a raised sanctuary area.*

A church outing to the seaside. The picture includes: Kathleen Coe and Charles 'Bar We' James.

THE CHURCH OF THE ASSUMPTION OF THE BLESSED VIRGIN MARY

The interior of the church prior to the Victorian makeover. Note the box pews and the pulpit halfway down the north wall of the church. The restoration work lasted over 30 years and these rare early pictures show the church in the late 1880s. (REPRODUCED BY PERMISSION OF RICHARD COE)

Looking into the chancel. The organ chamber has yet to be built and the hatchments of the Ray family of Plashwood hang on the walls. (REPRODUCED BY PERMISSION OF RICHARD COE)

Victorian makeover of the church, which also removed the box pews and the original pulpit. Fortunately, Richard Coe preserves the only known photographs from the pre-Victorian restoration period and these give a good picture of the box pews and the church as it was.

The pulpit was probably a triple-decker that allowed the vicar or rector to preach from the top level, the reader to read the scriptures from the middle level and the parish clerk to sit at the bottom, ground-floor level. He led the responses for the congregation.

To the rear of the church and above the vestry door are the hatchments. A hatchment was an apparently strange tradition, but you have to remember that it dates back to a time when many of the villagers would not have been able read or write, so there was no point displaying notices about deaths. Instead, for the more wealthy families, a board was made up, while the person was still alive, showing the coat of arms, which everyone locally would have recognised. Once the person died, the board was hung in a prominent place to announce the death.

Finally, let's look at the roof. It is a fine roof of alternate arch bracing and tie beams. It is very nicely decorated and probably dates back to the time when it was replaced after the clerestory was inserted in the 1450s. It has, however, been restored and here and there we can pick out areas of different shades of wood and different quality of carving. We also know that the roof was heavily restored in the Victorian period, when much other work was done in the church, and so it is difficult to date, without getting right up to the carvings and the timbers to find out exactly what has been replaced and what is original. The one thing of which we can be reasonably certain is that the restoration of the roof was completed in 1866 under the direction of the churchwardens W.

A hatchment of the Ray family.

Ebden and F. Andrews. How do we know? Well, they were kind enough to leave a record engraved into the timbers.

Let's now move up to the chancel steps, the division between the nave and the chancel. 'Nave' comes from the Latin 'navis' – a ship. The word 'chancel' comes from the Latin 'cancellus' meaning a screen. Originally there was a screen set up here to divide the chancel from the nave. This was known as the rood-screen because there was a 'rood' or 'cross' mounted on top of the screen. The screen stretched across the chancel arch and, at about the height of the column capitals, there was a walkway across, so that one of the assistants could light the candles on top of the screen.

These screens, and much of the more ornate decoration in the churches, were taken down over two periods. The first was at the time of the break from Rome in the 1450s. Anything that still survived was removed 100 years later under the supervision of William Dowsing.

Every church had a screen; it was an integral part of the service. The priest would enter by the priest's door into the chancel. He would put on his robes in the vestry or just in the chancel, taking the robes out of the robe or linen chest. He would then conduct much of the service from behind the screen and at the appropriate point the communicant members of the congregation would be allowed through the screen into the chancel to share the sacrament.

Because it is so high, few people notice the wonderful carvings in the nave roof.

St Mary's Church – note the path to the priest's door.

THE CHURCH OF THE ASSUMPTION OF THE BLESSED VIRGIN MARY

Although very few rood-screens still exist (one or two originals and a few rebuilt), in most churches it is hard to imagine that they were once there. However, if you know where to look you will find the traces. Looking at St Mary's chancel arches, the sawn-off ends of the main beams of the rood-screen are visible. On one side it has been conveniently used as a rawlplug to mount a reading lamp. Another tell-tale sign is the existence of a rood staircase – the narrow staircases found in some churches, winding up inside the wall or in one of the pillars. Usually it is just the remnant of the former staircase, sometimes used today as access to the hymn board. In other places they have been completely bricked in and plastered up so that no trace remains. At first glance you might think that Haughley is one such church where the staircase has been completely removed. However, look carefully behind the lectern and you can see quite clearly the outline of the archway that covered the entrance to the rood staircase. It would have opened out somewhere in the rough patch of plaster above and the staircase would have been enclosed, probably by building around the back of this column and into the corner of the south aisle. If you want to see what it looked like visit the screen that has been restored in Eye church, as it appears to be identical with the one that was in our church.

The area inside the screen, in the chancel, was the preserve of the priest and the patron of the church. As we mentioned earlier, it was the vicar (with or without a patron) who was responsible for the maintenance of the chancel. Only the clergy or the patron and his family could be buried in the chancel or have memorials put up for them. The clergy were buried with their feet to the west and the patron and his family with their feet to the east.

Again, it is difficult to be sure, but it seems likely that the organ niche was added in the Victorian period and the choir seating inserted. At the same time the barrel roof was inserted to try to improve the acoustics. If you stand in the nave and clap your hands there is no resonance. The acoustics are dead. This is not helped by our practice of placing all the kneelers on the backs of the pews – they deaden any resonance. In the chancel the Victorians tried to bring their music to life.

Just to the east of the organ is the outline of the early door that we could just discern from the outside; probably a door to the earlier vestry, or possibly the original priest's door, given that the approach from the original Vicarage was on that side of the church.

On the south wall of the chancel we have a fine, early piscina, contemporary with the building of this part of the church in 1300. There is, however, no sedilia, and this again points to the chancel being built rather later than the south aisle, where there is a sedilia. The piscina is quite low and this is because the floor of the sanctuary was raised during the Victorian restoration.

The altar rails are modern and not built for any other purpose than to serve as a suitable rest for the taking of communion. Altar rails were introduced in the mid-1600s at the order of Archbishop Laud, and they had a quite specific purpose. The rood-screens had been removed and in those days the church was much more open and used by the entire village. Dogs would run in and out and the altar rails were there to prevent the dogs from fouling the sanctuary area around the altar table. Again, in the pictures of Richard Coe, we can see the original Laudian altar rails that were removed in the nineteenth century.

During the 1990s many repairs have been necessary to prevent leaks and to prevent the tower from crumbling. The tower repairs in 1998/99 cost over £60,000, much of which was raised from the generous donations of grant-giving organisations such as the Suffolk Historic Churches Trust and from local individuals. However, the repair would not have been possible without a most generous bequest from Edith Eastall. At the same time the bells were removed from the tower and renovated and new headstocks were fitted.

Since then there has been a continuing battle against the ingress of damp and water, which is slowly being won; the remaining wooden floor at the rear of the church has been replaced because dry rot had taken hold; and urgent repairs have had to be carried out on some of the windows. In the winter of 2004/05 Rob Lewis undertook the restoration of the angels that decorate the roof of the south aisle.

Work on the church is closely controlled by the Diocese but every opportunity has been taken to make use of the abundant skills available within the village. The church has had the benefit of much time and effort from, among many, Dennis Spink, Richard Coe, Robert Stiff, Dennis Frost, Dennis Edwards and George Parry (long-time churchwarden who made the font cover which he presented to the church in 1979).

One of the embroidered kneelers in Haughley church. The Dean of Queen's College, Cambridge, was so impressed with the kneeler project that he commissioned kneelers for the College Chapel, which were made by the Haughley parishioners.

Above: *Richard Coe and Patrick Stephens repairing the bells and headstocks in 1999.*

Left: *One of the bells cast by Stefan Tonni of Bury St Edmunds in 1579.*

Below: *The old Vicarage, now the Grange, from the churchyard in 1930.*

✥ THE CHURCH OF THE ASSUMPTION OF THE BLESSED VIRGIN MARY ✥

One of the bells cast by Stefan Tonni of Bury St Edmunds in 1579.

Below: *One of the fine angels so expertly restored by Rob Lewis in 2005 – this one is playing a theobar, a cross between a lute and mandolin.*

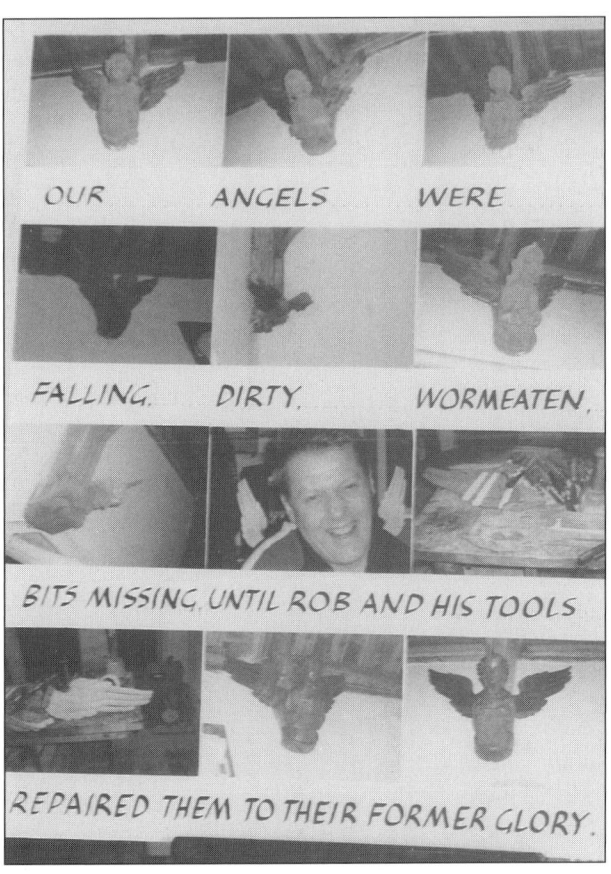

The poster created for the celebration to mark the restoration of the angels by Rob Lewis in 2005.

At the church gates in 1982 are Revd Douglas Sutch, churchwardens George Parry and Dudley Whittaker and lay elder Maurice Hart. Note the short war memorial, prior to its refurbishment.

THE CHURCH OF THE ASSUMPTION OF THE BLESSED VIRGIN MARY

Outside in the churchyard the grass is kept under control by the Faiers family – a thankless task as the grass seems to be growing at one end by the time they have finished the other! In recent years the grass in the older parts of the churchyard has been left to grow longer, which has allowed colourful spring flowers to flourish.

In 2005 the church is a busy and thriving part of the community. Revd Canon Deirdre Parmenter was the first female vicar of Haughley and has since also served a term as rural dean. The churchwardens, Josephine Gibson and Colin Hart, take a leading role in the maintenance and life of the church; the funds are in the care of the treasurer Howard Stephens, who took over from Jonathan Penn some five years ago, after Jonathan had undertaken the duty for the previous five years. The choir has blossomed under the expert guidance of Eileen Jones. Nesta Taylor has recently stood down from heading the fund-raising, although she still takes a very active interest. Gwen and Dennis Spink bring their valuable experience and expertise to the PCC. Pearl Wade seems ready to turn her hand to any task, and Celia Stephens has often headed the catering team. Dennis Frost is the tower captain and he heads a small team of bell-ringers who keep the bell-ringing tradition very much alive in the village. One could go on; there are so many who help in one way or another, but the important point is that the church is still very much at the heart of the community and many people spend time and resources in supporting it.

St Mary the Virgin is not the only religious establishment in Haughley. There is a United Reform church in Old Street and, because of the shape of the parish, many from Haughley New Street and Haughley Park find the Church of St Mary at Wetherden more convenient to attend. That church has been generously supported and endowed over the years by the occupants of Haughley Park, and from old maps and air photographs it appears that there was once a straight lane directly from the front of Haughley Park House to the church in Wetherden.

The United Reform church, or chapel as it was and still is called by some, was established in the village way back in 1679. In his history of the village, Revd MacCulloch notes a strange anomaly in that the licence to preach in the chapel, an off-shoot of the Congregational chapel in Stowmarket, was granted to Robert Hempson. But the same Robert Hempson was also churchwarden at St Mary the Virgin and had his children baptised there. In any event, the experiment did not last and it was not until 1843 that the present Nonconformist church was founded. Mr William Prentice and a group of colleagues were sent to spread the word in Haughley. The chapel was a popular alternative to the Established Church and it has survived since that day. Recently a combination of falling numbers in the congregation combined with the tragic death of the minister, Revd John Pugh, has caused activities to be reduced and there is a move to bring the two main churches in the village together.

At Haughley Green there is still a small gospel hall, previously called the Gospel Barn, where services used to be held for the Nonconformists led by Mr L.L.C. (Charlie) Betts. It closed in 2005.

Above: *An early flower festival in 1979.*

Above right: *Flowers in the chancel, 2005.*

Right: *Jack Stone's wedding at Haughley Green Gospel Hall. Included in the picture are: Peter Stone, Jack Stone, Winnie Hart, Mr Barker, John Hart, Phyllis Stone, Edie Hart, Freda Stone.*

The church choir in the 1930s. Left to right, back row: Ted Foy, Charlie Sore, Mr Green, Revd Grainge White, A. Whitehead, Walter Reynolds, Charlie Lambert, Aubrey Allum; third row: Enid Spink, Gwen Pleasance, Mrs Johnson, Anne Gladwell, Violet Gladwell, Belle Kemp, Minnie Nunn, Agnes Keeble, Miss Luckey, Arthur Creasy; second row (seated): Jack Keeble, Leslie Witherley, Reg Ager, Norman Reynolds, Frank Talbot, Douglas White, two Geaters (?); front row (seated on ground): Dennis Spink, Harold Spink, Clifford Haywood.

The Strict Baptist Association at Haughley Park in 1923. Left to right, back row: Herbert Whitehead, 'Farmer' Whitehead, Maud Whitehead, Sam Whitehead, Albert Mothersole; middle row: Mrs Stannard, Kathleen Rushbrooke, Caroline Hammond, Hattie Rushbrooke, Ethel Ling; front: Olive Stannard.

THE CHURCH OF THE ASSUMPTION OF THE BLESSED VIRGIN MARY

Haughley Green Gospel Hall Sunday school's outing to Felixstowe in 1920s. The adults include: George Fellingham, Jack Dorling, Doris Dorling (née Lingley), John and Martin Hart, Will Dorling, Mrs Edgar Fellingham, Walter Dorling, Bertie Hart. The children at the front include: Gwen Pleasance, Ada Bloss, Edie Hart, Maurice Hart, Lenny Murton, Cecil Woods, Bert Aldous.

Flowers in the chancel for the flower festival in 1979.

A boy pushes his bike up the hill towards Plashwood in 1900.

A horse and cart passing Folly House, c.1930.

Richard Coe with his 'Cyclomotor' delivery bike. These bikes were known as 'winged wheels' from their advertising slogan; 'Winged wheel gives power to your heel'.

Chapter Six

Transport in Haughley

Bill Green

The main routes through the region in 2005 mostly link the Midlands with the ports of Felixstowe and Harwich. The east–west flow of traffic is enormous and has led to the need to enhance the A14 road. The road acts almost as a barrier and divides the county into north and south areas. But it was not always like that. The Romans had established themselves at Colchester and the links from Colchester ran up to Norwich (the A140 being a distinctive road of Roman origin), Burgh and Dunwich and travel beyond the region was either to London or along the line of Claydon, Ixworth, King's Lynn and Lincoln. Thus the main routes ran north–south. Any westward travel would have been via Bury St Edmunds to join the Norwich–London road to travel southwards.

Horse, cart or foot were the only early options and there is no doubt that people were fitter and stronger than they are today, and were quite capable of walking 35 to 40 miles in a day for days on end. However, the need to travel was rare and most movements were either military or in support of the early trade. For most day-to-day items the area was self-sufficient and many villagers would never venture beyond the village during their lifetime. Thus it stayed for many hundreds of years for, like many similar villages, Haughley had little to commend it in terms of communication. Then came the railways, the power of steam and the internal-combustion engine. Previously, goods coming in and out of the village would have been transported by packhorse and horse or hand-drawn cart.

However, when the power of steam appeared Haughley's location on the 'new' railway network, betwixt Ipswich, Norwich and Cambridge, enabled a new station known as Haughley Junction to become established in 1849. This was on the then Eastern Union Railway, later to become the Great Eastern Railway in 1862 when other small East Anglian railway companies combined to create the GER. This enabled those within Haughley to commute easily to all parts of the region and beyond.

There was no apparent reason for early development of the railway into this backwater of England that was comparatively untouched by the industrial revolution, and yet the railways made their first appearance surprisingly early. However, the completion of the network took a long time and many branch lines either never left the drawing-board or were left partially completed.

Norfolk and Suffolk had no major trading ports, there were no great centres of industry. Therefore, there was arguably no reason to invest in railway communications, the payback for which might never be achieved. Nevertheless, as early as 1836 an Act was passed permitting the construction of a railway line from London to Colchester. The Eastern Counties Railway set about building the line, no doubt with the aim of going on to Harwich, Ipswich and Norwich. By 1843 they had reached Colchester but the several years of investment had left the company short of cash and they were unable to fund further work. The Eastern Union took up the challenge and by 1846 had extended the line to Ipswich.

Haughley had been a thriving small market settlement in the sixteenth and seventeenth centuries. It was well placed for communications, sitting astride routes that had developed from Ipswich to Bury St Edmunds and from Colchester to Thetford and Lynn.

The signal-box at Haughley Junction in 1926.

Horses queue outside the Forge in the 1930s.

R. W. ARMSTRONG (HAUGHLEY) LTD.

Automobile Engineers

NEW STREET GARAGE
HAUGHLEY

STOWMARKET - SUFFOLK

TELEPHONE: ELMSWELL 314

Directors:
R. W. G. ARMSTRONG
V. M. ARMSTRONG
R. C. LAFLIN
J. S. LAFLIN

Customers' Cars stored or driven at owner's risk

Mr. R. Coe.
Old Street.
Haughley.
Stowmarket.

31st. Jan. 1969.

Nov. 6   To Account Rendered.   £1. 18. 6d.

✦ TRANSPORT IN HAUGHLEY ✦

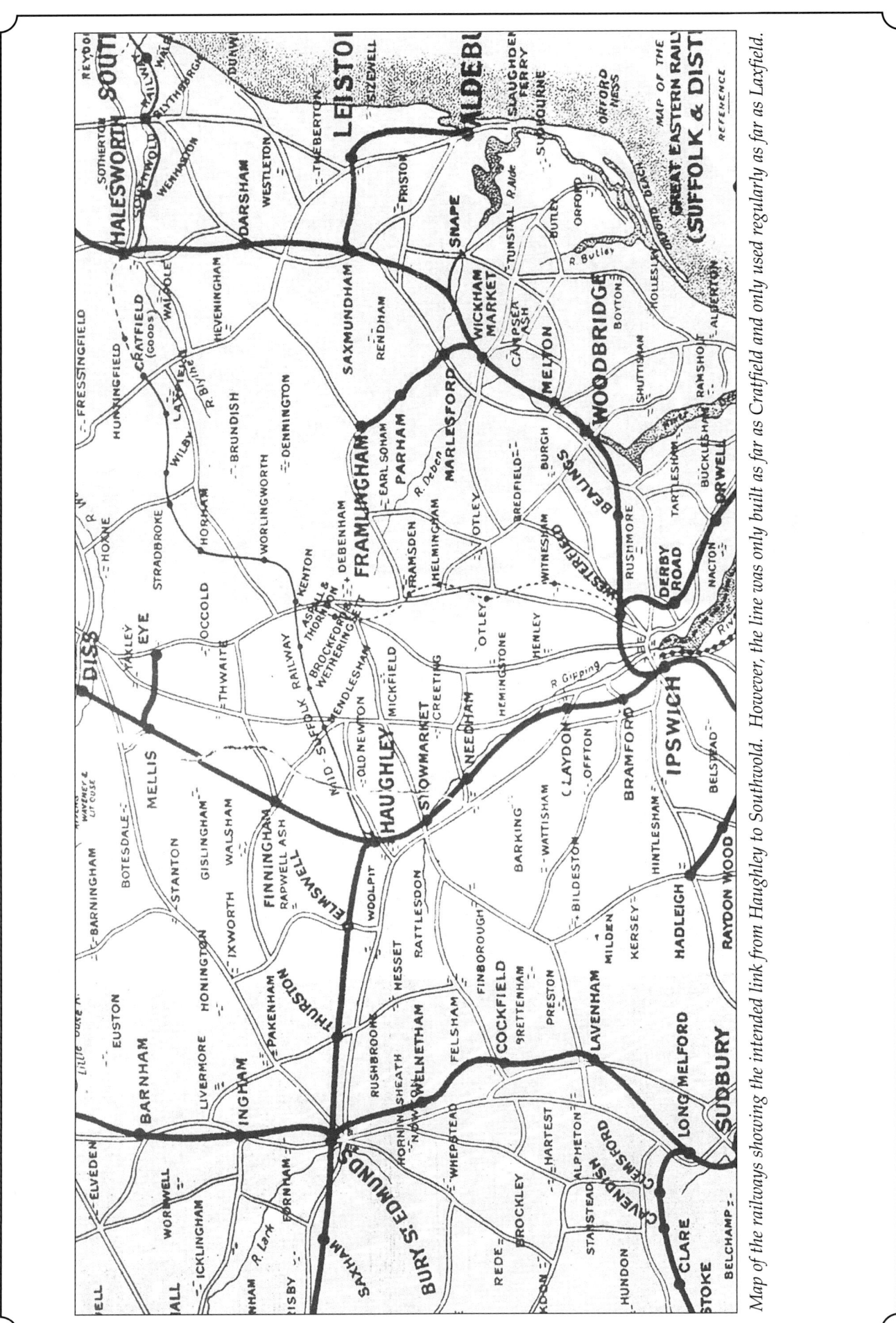

Map of the railways showing the intended link from Haughley to Southwold. However, the line was only built as far as Cratfield and only used regularly as far as Laxfield.

It had its own docks at Dagworth and was just a couple of miles from Stowmarket and then, via Bramford, to Ipswich. When the Ipswich & Bury Railway Company built a line from Ipswich to Stowmarket (July 1845) and then on to Bury in 1846, Haughley Station was built, within easy walking distance of the village centre and Haughley Green, adjacent to the bridge on the road between Haughley and Haughley Green. Remember, of course, that Haughley at that time was concentrated in Old Street, Duke Street and the Folly. There was very little development beyond the bottom of Old Street. The half mile to the bridge on Haughley Green Road would have been along a peaceful cart track and the villagers would have thought themselves well-served by the new facility that could take them rapidly to Bury St Edmunds or to Ipswich and London.

The first timetables show that the journey time from London to Ipswich was 80 minutes, and to Haughley, 94 minutes – not bad when you consider that it still takes 80 minutes today and trains would have had many more stops along the way.

If this had been the end of the story perhaps Haughley would have prospered and grown. However, in early 1847, when the Ipswich & Bury Railway merged with the Eastern Union Railway, they started to build the line from Ipswich to Norwich. The first stretch to Haughley already existed, but here they divided the line and headed north to Finningham, Burston and finally to Norwich Victoria Station (later to Thorpe Station). The line was completed on 7 November 1849.

The problem for Haughley was that the original station, convenient for the village, was the wrong side of the new Haughley Junction. It clearly would have been nonsense to have to go to Stowmarket and change trains if you wanted to go to Norwich, and so a new station that could serve both the Norwich and the Bury routes was constructed at the junction. The original station was dismantled after a short working life of just three years, although parts are still visible

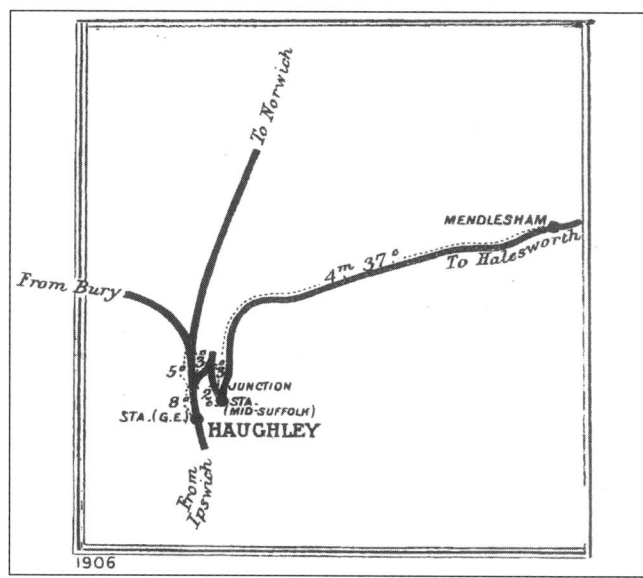

A plan of Haughley Junction from 1906, shortly after the opening of the Mid-Suffolk Light Railway.

Haughley Junction Station, which actually stood outside the parish in Old Newton, 1950. The original name of the station was Haughley Road (Old Newton), but the locals insisted on calling it Haughley Junction and eventually the Great Eastern Railway gave up and renamed it.

to this day and the main building has been converted into a pleasant house.

The new station was originally called Haughley Road, reflecting the fact that it was not in Haughley but on the road to Haughley. However, it was called Haughley Junction by all the locals and eventually the railway company gave up and changed its name to Haughley Junction in 1890. The point was that Haughley no longer had easy access to the station, which was now a good mile walk from the village – hence the downturn in village fortunes. It was almost as quick to walk to Stowmarket!

However, in railway terms the junction was very important. It was a station where passengers changed trains and where freight was marshalled, but in particular it was the exchange point for the night mails. Mail from London, Norwich, Peterborough and the Continent via Harwich, was exchanged for onward movement. The trains were directed onto a loop to keep the main line clear whilst the mailbags were transferred or the mail vans were unhitched from one train and hitched to another.

Its role as a junction increased with the opening of the Mid-Suffolk Light Railway or 'Middy' as it was affectionately called. Milk, produce and schoolchildren used the Middy to Haughley and then changed trains for onward movement to Stowmarket and Ipswich. To cope with the through traffic of trains, freight and passengers, Haughley Station had substantial and extensive buildings that remained in use until 1967. There were six platforms, a footbridge, several sidings, two signal-boxes, grain sidings, a goods shed, a goods yard, a turntable and the level crossing. An enormous multi-storey grain drier was built alongside in 1950. In 2005, the grain drier remains, as does a small remnant of the original booking-hall, but as one crosses the level crossing there is nothing else to see.

TRANSPORT IN HAUGHLEY

J15 locomotive on its way from Haughley to Laxfield, c.1930.

Haughley never benefited from the railway in the way that other towns and villages with direct access to the railway prospered. Trains no longer stop at Haughley and the associated infrastructure has disappeared.

The Middy was a typical example of a branch line. Like many it was built at the turn of the century to serve the villages and agriculture of the region. Haughley Junction Station was enlarged in 1903 to cope with its additional role as the terminus for the line. It was never envisaged that the Middy would carry heavy locomotives and traffic and so the line was built to light standards to Mendlesham, Brockford, Kenton, Aspall and Laxfield. The railway opened in 1904 and was later extended as far as Cratfield for freight only. The original plan was to create a link across to Southwold to provide a rail service from the Midlands through to the Suffolk coast. It was also planned to create a further link with the East Suffolk Railway, which ran via Debenham and Otley to Ipswich, but these links were never built.

The Mid-Suffolk wanted to share the station facility at Haughley Junction and approached the Great Eastern Railway to ask them to arrange the necessary enlargement. The Great Eastern quoted such an enormous sum that the Middy took fright and decided to build their own station adjacent to the existing station. In the official records the two stations are shown as Haughley East for the Middy and Haughley West for the GER, but in practice the locals grouped the two together and continued to call them Haughley Junction. The new station was skilfully built to give the impression of a substantial station but it was actually a timber frame covered with zinc sheets and then well painted. It might almost have been the prototype for the old Hornby tin-plate model station!

Sadly, and again like many of the branch lines, it was difficult to make ends meet. The extension to Cratfield closed after just six years. The cattle docks that had been provided at every station were never properly used and they fell into disrepair. They were soon scrapped as corn started to replace cattle as the main agricultural focus in the area. A start had been made on the link to Kenton and Debenham but, as raw materials became scarce during the First World War, it was decided to lift the part of the line that had been laid, because the materials were wanted for more important purposes. This effectively destroyed any plans for completing the original scheme.

The Middy stumbled along but was never a profitable affair. In 1924 it was officially taken over, along with the Great Eastern Railway, by the London and North Eastern Railway (LNER) but the LNER showed no interest in this 'backwater' and the Middy continued to operate virtually independently. The only change on which the LNER insisted was the closure of the Middy terminus, Haughley East, and centralisation on the old GER station. The Middy terminus was flattened.

From a driver's point of view, the Middy also presented a few challenges. The line out of Haughley was up an exacting 1 in 43 gradient and, with no run at the slope, it was a good test of both locomotive and

Building the bridge to carry the Middy over Haugh Lane in 1902. The structure proved to be weak and was largely rebuilt c.1940.

A Claude Hamilton class locomotive climbs Haughley Bank in February 1951.

✧ TRANSPORT IN HAUGHLEY ✧

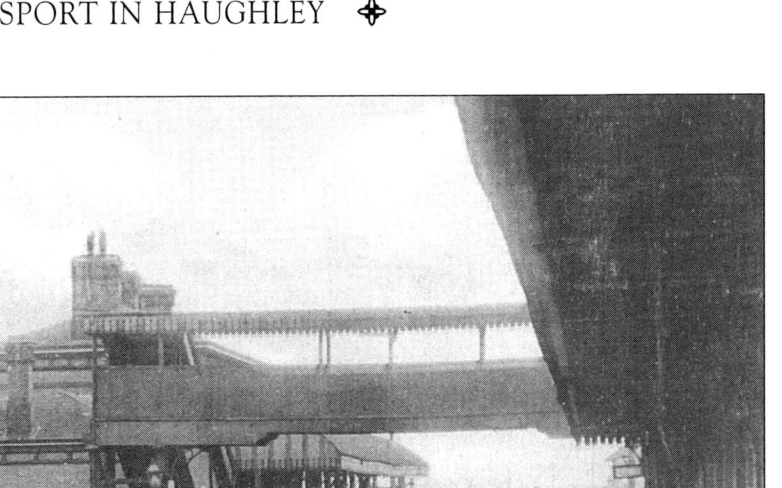

Haughley Junction Station, 1909.

driver. However, it was the return journey on which more problems occurred. A 'runaway' train coming down the gradient could never have stopped and there was always the risk that a train might crash through the terminus at Haughley and onto the main line. There are several recorded incidents of trains overshooting at Haughley but fortunately none were serious. To try to minimise the risk strict weight limits were applied – whilst the up trains were allowed to haul 21 wagons, the down trains were limited to 14.

At first the Middy provided a part-time service, running on just three days a week for both passengers and freight. This was increased to a daily train in the sugar-beet season and the trains were usually mixed passenger and freight. In 1920 a daily passenger service was introduced, largely to carry schoolchildren, and at its peak four trains were run each way for six days a week, with just one train each way on Sundays. The Middy, and most of the other branch lines, never really grew up in terms of operating infrastructure, and there was an unmistakable air of self-help and improvisation about these little railways. The Middy had just two signals on the entire line and these were at Haughley. The level-crossing gates, of which there were several between Haughley and Laxfield, were all opened and closed by the train crew themselves. The timetable was flexible with an estimated travelling time of between 64 and 75 minutes to complete a journey along the full length of the line.

The Middy had a slight resurgence during the Second World War when it was used to move munitions and supplies for some of the Suffolk airbases, but after the war use dwindled. It survived the 1948 nationalisation, but only just, and in 1952 it was closed. Nature and agriculture between them quickly reclaimed the trackbed and within a few years it was almost impossible to trace the route of the railway. A keen map reader and observer might still be able to find a few traces here and there, but even along the Middy footpath it is difficult to imagine that trains once ran along the same route.

There is, however, a good collection of local anecdotes from the days of steam trains, not just relating to the time when the Middy overran and crashed through the level-crossing gates. Mr W.F. Windham, or 'Mad Windham' as he was known, was of aristocratic blood and lived at Felbrigg Hall in Norfolk. He was an exuberant young man who enjoyed a joke, and to this end he developed the habit of dressing up in the uniform of the railway company and impersonating the officials. In mid-1861 he effectively highjacked the train at Haughley, where he took over as guard. The train moved down to Stowmarket where Windham signalled for the train to move off before the passengers had finished boarding. Several were thrown back onto the platform and there were many injuries.

In 1874 George Rands established what was probably a first – he was arrested at Haughley after being

'Out of steam', a locomotive breaches the end of the Mid-Suffolk Light Railway in a field at Cratfield. The line was closed in July 1952.

An E4 class locomotive, 62785, near Haughley (but not on the Middy), 30 July 1957 (now preserved at Bressingham Steam Museum as GER490).

TRANSPORT IN HAUGHLEY

A class J39 locomotive hauls a goods train southwards through Haughley Junction, 1955.

Old Street in the snow, 1993. (PHOTOGRAPH GEOFF CLARKE)

A spectacular accident at Haughley Junction in 1955. Fortunately no one was seriously injured. The subsequent inquiry found that there had been a mechanical failure of the points. (G.R. WILDEN)

involved in a noisy and unpleasant argument on the train. Rands had insisted on smoking in a non-smoking compartment and his fellow passengers complained. Rands refused to stop smoking and a scuffle ensued. He was arrested by the station staff who held him until the police arrived.

Working the night mails obviously had its effect on one of the local porters who apparently dozed off in church. A kindly neighbour nudged him to wake him up before the vicar noticed, and the porter promptly leapt to his feet in the middle of the church service and announced 'Haughley, Haughley – change here for Finningham, Mellis and all stations to Norwich'.

Haughley Junction was an important railway station both in war and peacetime. Farmers were able to transport crops such as sugar beet and corn to market, mills and processing plants economically. The early commuters could easily access their place of work and holidaymakers were able to find their way to the seaside and other holiday destinations, not forgetting the shopper or visitor who could get in and out of Haughley easily.

Boat trains travelling from Liverpool to Harwich Parkeston Quay, via Ely, Lincoln, Sheffield and Manchester, plus a number of stations in between and on to the Hook of Holland and Zeebrugge, passed through Haughley, being a popular method of journeying from port to port and on to the continent of Europe. The very first boat trains ran in 1883, finally ceasing cross-country during 1987 when air travel became popular, thus killing off what was to many a romantic method of travel. However, even in 2005 travel to Harwich can be made by train through Haughley, but all must change at Ipswich and a boat train still runs from Liverpool Street Station, London to Harwich Parkeston Quay, but it cannot conjure up the nostalgia of yesteryear, when the steam-powered boat trains ran across our country, safely delivering their passengers.

During the Second World War Haughley Junction became one of the hubs for the supply of ordinance to the British and American Air Force bases that proliferated this area. Trains brought bombs from armament factories in the industrial Midlands and North of England, which were then transported by road to various airfields for use against the enemy. One story tells the incident of a trailer carrying munitions from Haughley Station proceeding down Station Road, losing control and shedding its cargo at Cock Corner. Fortunately none of the weapons were armed, so all lived to tell the tale!

Another tale tells of a passenger who alighted the train at Stowmarket for Cambridge and learned, very soon after the train left the station, that it was in fact destined for Norwich. Alerting the conductor of the mistake, the train made an unscheduled halt at Haughley Junction to enable the passenger to leave the incorrect train and then catch the next train heading in the direction of Cambridge – old values of courtesy that would perhaps be hard to find in the twenty-first century!

Sadly, Haughley Junction was closed as a working station during in the 1960s and all that remains is the unmanned crossing and memories.

Just to the south of Haughley lies what some call the longest dock road in the country – the A14. This major trunk road connects the ports of Felixstowe and Harwich with the North of England and the Midlands. It also connects, via the A11 just to the west of Newmarket, to the M11 to the south-east, London and southern ports such as Southampton and Portsmouth. Today this road is some 130 miles long. The A14 began as most major roads, a stage and mail-coach route, connecting Ipswich to Bury St Edmunds and beyond. Whilst the village of Haughley was not directly on the stagecoach route, it did in fact run through Haughley New Street. No substantial records can be located regarding this route, but it is known that the first coaches ran from 1787 – this was the second area in the country to have such a coaching route. Coaching inns at Wetherden, Woolpit and Barham are still found by the roadside, as also is the occasional milestone.

The records show that there was a toll station at Squire's Cross, where taxes for use of the road would have been collected by the lord of the manor.

When the motor vehicle appeared as the favoured method of travel and transporting goods, the mail-coach routes became macadam roads and the Bury Road, as it was known in those days, became the A45, which for the most part connected every town and village on its route towards the Great North Road, now the A1(M). A typical journey from Haughley to the Great North Road could take three hours to complete. During the 1970s a new A45 was built in stages to bypass those towns and villages, and the longest dual carriageway in East Anglia was completed. When a new dual carriageway section was completed and opened in August 1991 from the A1(M) in Cambridgeshire to the M1/M6 junction on the Northamptonshire and Warwickshire borders, the A45 became known as the A14. This new highway was not without its faults and whilst there were many changes along the route the infamous Haughley Bends remained and became a notorious accident black spot. In 2005 the daily traffic volume is in excess of 38,000 vehicles, 20 per cent of which are heavy-goods vehicles, and this figure is rising with the increasing expansion of Felixstowe and Harwich docks.

Sadly, many drivers and passengers and some pedestrians have been killed and maimed just a few hundred yards from our village. The sound of a police car or ambulance siren attending to an accident on the 'Bends' is an all-too-common sound, heard coming from the direction of the A14. During the year 2000 a 50mph safety restriction was imposed and speed cameras installed to 'catch' those who speed through this dangerous section of road. The speed limit has reduced accidents by 50 per cent. Over the past two years (since 2003) the Highways Agency has been proposing a realignment of the A14 and a new junction for better and safer access on to and off this major trunk road. A public consultation took place during early 2003 with an exhibition of the possibilities for alternative alignments and junctions. Following this the preferred route was announced in March 2004. The chosen solution was one that places the new roadway section further to the south of the existing carriageway, with access to and from the A14 by means of a two-level separated interchange at a point close to Tothill. The contract was awarded to Birse Civils, a major UK contractor, during March 2005. This contract is an 'early contractor involvement' type being a design and

No need for speed humps in 1904.

Nora Plummer in the 1920s, in one of the village's early cars.

Cecil and Len Murton at Murton's Garage, Haughley Green, c.1930.

A charabanc outing of an unknown organisation in the 1920s.

TRANSPORT IN HAUGHLEY

A ladies' charabanc outing, possibly the Haughley WI, c.1930.

Murton's Garage, Haughley Green, with Cecil and Charlie Murton, c.1930.

A 'locomobile' car enters the village in 1904. No problem parking near the Post Office then!

The road through Haughley New Street, then the main Bury St Edmunds to Stowmarket road, blocked by snow in 1954. (W.G. WILDEN)

❖ TRANSPORT IN HAUGHLEY ❖

Above: *Snow in Duke Street, 1950.*

Above left: *The petrol station at Haughley Green, c.1950.*

Left: *Coaches form up by the village green for an outing to the seaside in the 1950s. Fred Harper, John Turner, Aubrey Allum and Mr Birch pose by their coach.*

Palmer's Bakery van parked on the village green in the 1950s. (PHOTOGRAPH C. BOURNE)

build award. Under this type of contract the contractor discusses all aspects of the project with the local councils, to ensure that all affected parties benefit from its completion. Early proposals seem to show that the new section will bring great benefits to the village of Haughley, with much improved access, traffic-noise reduction levels and an underpass connecting Haughley with Harleston, to allow access between the villages without crossing the carriageway. A further spin-off of this underpass will be that it will provide a safe crossing place for deer, badgers and other mammals which all too often are casualties of speeding traffic on the A14. One of the existing carriageways will be left as an access/service road to Haughley, Haughley Green and Haughley New Street, and the other will be reduced in width to become a walkway and cycle route. A full exhibition of proposals is expected to take place towards the end of 2005 for further public comment. Depending on the outcome of this exhibition, the completion of the A14 contract is expected during 2008. This cannot come soon enough for many villagers.

A bus service began running from Tothill, Haughley, owned and operated by the Eastern Counties Road Car Company. In 1931 this became the Eastern Counties Bus Company, when it conjoined with the Ortona Motor Company of Cambridge, the United Automobile Service of Lowestoft and the Peterborough Electric Traction Company. This new enterprise was begun because the 1931 Road Traffic Act stated that all bus services had to be licensed. Buses did not begin to enter the village for many years, so there was still a need to walk out of the village along Fishponds Way to Tothill to catch a bus to Stowmarket or Bury St Edmunds.

We cannot be sure who owned the very first motor car in Haughley but pictures exist of a 1904 'locomobile' in the village (see page 94), so it seems the car came quite early. The first commercial vehicle would have been owned by the Palmer family – the village bakers – and was used for delivering products further afield. It goes without saying that, at that time, only the gentry could afford motor cars, and even as late as the early 1950s a boy's pastime would be guessing the make of the next car to pass on the A45 at Tothill. Even here, on the main road, this 'new' form of transport was not such a regular occurrence.

And finally, was Haughley ever connected to the sea via the River Gipping? Well not quite Haughley, but perhaps Dagworth was, within the parish of Haughley. Back in 1789 a William Jessop, a canal builder of repute, was commissioned by a group of six local landowners (the trustees) to survey the River Gipping valley, with a view to making the river navigable. Following his survey he presented evidence to a Parliamentary Committee who were considering the Bill of Navigation. Shortly afterwards he prepared drawings and specifications to be used for the basis of tenders, and was given Royal Assent on 1 April 1790, under the then Act (Act 30th George III. Cap 57). Within three years the 'Act 33rd George III. Cap 20, Royal Assent 28th March 1793' was approved and construction began immediately. It was completed in 1798, at a cost of £14,300, with a further sum of £6,000 set aside if necessary, on mortgage or by granting annuities. Henceforth the Ipswich & Stowmarket Navigation Company was born. The length of this canal was some 17 miles from the tideway at Stoke Bridge, Ipswich, on and through Stowmarket via 15 locks, with a further extension of ¾ mile from Stowupland Bridge to Dagworth. The purpose of the canal was to transport corn and other grain, hops, stone, timber, goods, wares, merchandise and other things, except coal, at a rate of 1d. per ton. Coal was to be transported at a rate of ½d. per ton. Vessels of less than 35 tons laden would be charged as if they were 35 tons. Interestingly, manure being transported seems to have gone for free! Navigation flourished with up to 30 journeys being made weekly, although these took some 16 hours per round trip. However, the coming of rail in 1844 and the new Haughley Junction in 1849 caused many problems for the navigation with a reduction in use, thus the trustees negotiated with the railway which rented the navigation for 42 years, a wise decision as dividends were freely paid. In 1888 the railway refused to renegotiate the agreement so the navigation company took back the running of a then declining business. By 1890 the navigation virtually ceased trading. The Ipswich & Stowmarket Navigation Company was finally wound up in 1929, perhaps around the time the first trucks made their appearance on our roads. Some 76 years later modern versions of those trucks can be seen thundering along the A14 daily in their thousands.

Caroline Bowden, Sharon Pirrie, Judy Frost, Maurice Hart, Dennis Frost, Colin Hart, June Paddy and Mike Pirrie listen to the pre-flight briefing before taking a balloon trip from the Playing Field, 3 August 1999.

Chapter Seven
Farming in Haughley
Gerard Artingdale and Marion Wilson

Haughley, like most rural communities, owes its existence to farming, in a relationship that goes back to before the Norman Conquest. Haughley Castle dates back to Saxon times, and although the settlement arguably grew up around the castle, the village survived the loss of its castle in the twelfth century.

During the early Middle Ages farming in Haughley would have been carried out mainly by peasants, who had small surpluses to sell or exchange for food. In 1227 this had become sufficient for a market to be set up on the village green. Haughley was the centre of a densely populated area growing crops and rearing livestock for food.

The Black Death of 1348 caused a major change in the farming landscape. With the population diminished there was no longer such demand for food, nor the workers to produce it. Lower returns and higher labour costs caused a switch to more pastoral farming. In this area the wool trade developed, and became England's most important export commodity.

A number of today's farms can trace their roots back to the Middle Ages and were then probably dedicated to the wool trade. The wealth of farms and manors in the area can be seen by the number that had moats dug around them, with those at New Bells Farm, Wassicks Farm and Wetherden Hall still surviving in 2005. The reason for these moats is not entirely clear, as they rarely encircle the buildings so were not for defence from raiders. It is possible that some at least were dug for reasons of prestige by aspiring landed gentry, or more prosaically because moats gave a more reliable source of water.

These ancient farms were the first to benefit from the enclosure of common land. Enclosure was the conversion of the medieval open-field system of farming into that of enclosed fields surrounded by hedges or ditches. What had been common land became private property. This process took hundreds of years to complete, and as late as 1842 the land both sides of the road through Haughley Green remained as common.

As a result of this process of enclosure, by the middle of the nineteenth century almost all of the farms that are still operating in 2005, or retain the title of 'farm' in their name, were in existence. In all there were nearly 20 farms in the parish, although until 1966 Red House Farm was actually in Old Newton not Haughley. Some of the names and many of the boundaries have changed. Boggis's Farm is

Mr Musk and Mr Pearl with their thistlehooks near the Grove at Wetherden Hall Farm, c.1900.

now Green Farm, whilst the original Green Farm, rather confusingly, is now Laurel Farm, and Belle Vue became Orchard Farm.

Even if the names are familiar, the landscape would have been quite different from that which we see today. The early-twenty-first-century, largely arable, farms would have been predominantly mixed farms with livestock, fruit and hops growing alongside arable fields. The actual mix within the farm would have depended on the type of soil found there. This varies from heavy clay in the north to light sandy soil in the south. In Haughley Park the soil is so sandy it is doubtful whether it has ever been cultivated, and would have been used solely for grazing.

The other striking difference in today's farming, compared with that of any period from the Middle Ages is that in the past the fields would have been a hive of activity. Before the arrival of motor vehicles farming was a horse-drawn, labour-intensive activity. It was not until 1953 that Gordon Stiff of Mere Farm became the first local farmer to own a combine harvester. However, 30 years earlier the internal combustion engine was a contributory factor to the biggest depression to hit farming.

Above: 'Farmer' (Herbert) Whitehead and Herbert Coe (blacksmith) cutting hay on what is now the Playing Field, 1935.

Left: Bob Baldry harvesting at Wiseman's (now Red House) Farm in the 1930s.

Below: A local passenger train passes harvesters at Haugh Farm, c.1920. Left to right: Littleton Whitehead, Jane Whitehead, Veronica Whitehead, Kate Whitehead, Maud Whitehead.

A 'dish of tea' to keep the hedging party warm on a winter's day, 1950s. The picture includes: *Fred Harper* (standing with cap), *'Stub' Arbon* (seated third from left).

Herbert Hart with his homemade cab on the tractor at Mrs Lingley's farm at Old Hall, Haughley Green, c.1939.

Above: *Mabel Harper and Kate Pryke, with Hilda Pryke as a small child, join the harvesters in the 1920s.*

Left: *Connie McKenna with a basket of fruit at Wiseman's (now Red House) Farm. Connie came from Woolwich every summer for a number of years.*

Below: *Staff of the Soil Association, 1949–51, at Walnut Tree Manor. Left to right, back row: Ben Easey, Philip Denny, Harold Cropp, Mrs Hurst, Arthur Aldous; front row: Tom Puzey, Helen MacLeod, Paddy Hurst, Eileen Girling, Anne Medley, Zena Bullett.*

The farm cottages on Plashwood Road. (PHOTOGRAPH RICHARD COE)

FARMING IN HAUGHLEY

The Depression proper hit in the 1930s, but farmers were hit by a number of other factors. Competition from the prairies of America is usually cited as one of these, but another, that is often forgotten, is that prior to the First World War nearly a quarter of land under production was dedicated to providing fodder and supplies for horses. With the advent of cars and trucks demand for this collapsed. The extent to which this impacted Haughley is shown by the bankruptcies of Wassicks, Haugh, and Walnut Tree Farms, which were sold to Lady Eve Balfour of New Bells Farm for just 2s.6d. (now 12.5p) an acre.

Haugh, sometimes known as Hoo, Farm was, until its bankruptcy in 1931, owned by the Whitehead family, one of the mainstays of the village. Kruger Whitehead is mentioned elsewhere in this book. His brother Herbert John was known to all as Farmer Whitehead.

The farms in Haughley were also subject to the tithe system. This was a charge levied by the Church on farmers' crops. The fall in prices in the 1930s meant that this tax became disproportionate to income, and many were unable or unwilling to pay. In order to enforce the tithe the Church Commissioners sent in bailiffs, and farmers banded together to resist. The bailiffs hired more men to help them enforce the tithes, and thus began what became known as the Tithe War. In 1934 the bailiffs arrived in Haughley accompanied by 30 black-shirted supporters of Oswald Mosley's Fascist party, to carry out a dawn raid on New Bells Farm. Despite her livestock being forcibly confiscated, the publicity surrounding this attack on Lady Eve Balfour led to the setting up of a Royal Commission and abolition of the tithe.

It is perhaps not so widely appreciated that Haughley, or to be accurate, Haughley Green, can lay claim to being the birthplace of the organic movement. In 1940 the Haughley Research Trust, under the leadership of Lady Eve Balfour, began organic farming trials on her farms at Haughley Green. The initial results of these trials were published in 1943 in her book *The Living Soil*. This received such interest and acclaim that by 1946 the book had been reprinted and revised five times, and led to Lady Eve becoming the first chairwoman of the newly founded Soil Association. This organisation became and still is the UK's leading campaigner for organic food and farming.

The 'Haughley Experiment', as it became known, continued until 1969, and Walnut Tree Manor (now Hillcroft Preparatory School) remained the national headquarters of the Soil Association until 1971.

It is a pity, however, that the impact of this work on the people of Haughley who worked for Lady Eve and for the Soil Association, is not more widely recorded, an omission which is probably accidentally reflected in the lack, other than the naming of Eve Balfour Way, of any lasting memorial in Haughley to this pioneering work.

Spencer Gladwell and Reg Faiers bringing in the hay at Dial Farm, c.1939.

If it was difficult to make a living out of farming in the pre-war period, life was, as it had always been, much harder for the farm workers. It is hard to imagine now that many of the present-day cottages in Haughley were then subdivided and home to families living five or more to a bedroom. Wages fell by half in the early 1920s and it took the arrival of the Second World War for fortunes to improve for both farmers and workers.

During the war the shortage of labour caused by the drafting of men into the Forces was offset by Land Girls, some of whom married and stayed in Haughley after the war. Labour was also provided by Italian prisoners of war from the camp at Plashwood.

The ups and downs of the farming industry have meant that very few of Haughley's farms have been in the same family for any length of time. A notable exception is Dial Farm, which has been owned by the Faiers family since the mid-1700s. At one time this farm provided milk for the delivery service to the village. Also, Plashwood has been in the Bevan family for more than 100 years. In the 1960s the estate ran 200 milking cows, a beef herd, 6,000 broiler chickens and 70 sows. It is now entirely arable.

The corollary to this lack of longevity of ownership has been an influx of farmers from outside the village – from Eric Noy of Red House Farm who moved just a mile or so from Gipping, to George Bryson of Rookery Farm who came down from Ayrshire, and to farthest away of all, the Australian-born Gordon Stiff of Mere Farm.

Top: *Loading hay in Haughley, c.1912.*

Above: *Ploughing by tractor in the 1920s.*

Below: *Sheep shearing at Haughley Green in the 1930s.*

Kruger Whitehead, pictured in 1920 with his dog and gun. The Whitehead family had farmed at Haugh Farm but Kruger became the landlord of the White Horse, Haughley New Street, and then the King's Arms between 1936 and 1961. In a competition of Greene King landlords in 1952 he was the winner for naming a new beer – Abbot Ale.

FARMING IN HAUGHLEY

Loading hay from what is now the Playing Field, c.1919.

Taking a break. Left to right: Bob Wilding, Mr Green and Mr Ranson.

Walnut Tree Manor as it was advertised in the sale particulars that attracted Lady Eve Balfour. In 2005 it is called Walnutree Manor and is used as Hillcroft Preparatory School.

New Bells Farm from the air, 1951.

Victor Plummer with a rabbit, c.1940.

Pippy Faiers, as a babe in arms, taking an early ride behind a tractor, driven by Spencer Gladwell.

Working horses at rest, Haughley Green.

Above: *In the harvest field at Red House Farm, 1927.*

Above right: *A cart load of hay.*

Far right: *Pond dredging, c.1930.*

Right: *Bob Baldry feeding a pig at Wiseman's (now Red House) Farm 1935*

Gordon Stiff bought Mere Farm in 1952 and introduced hop plants, as there was a disease affecting hops in Kent – the traditional home of hops. At one time he was cultivating up to 250,000 hop plants, along with strawberries, raspberries, as well as breeding pigs and cattle. In 2005, Gordon having retired from hop growing, the farm is arable.

Hops had been grown between Haughley and Stowmarket during the eighteenth and for much of the nineteenth centuries. There remains the lower section of an oast house in Spike's Lane, and osier beds also existed in this area.

Eric Noy and his father John bought Red House Farm in 1966 from the Wiseman family. Since the 1920s this had been a fruit farm growing apples, plums, strawberries, etc., with sugar beet, potatoes and wheat. Over the years the balance changed, and the Noys diversified further in order to offer bed and breakfast accommodation. They also developed a caravan site.

At the time of writing the Common Agricultural Policy is being revised to better reward environmental stewardship of the countryside. The impact this will have on landscape and farms in and around the Haughley over the next few years is unlikely to have as much impact as an unrealised plan, drawn up in the 1960s, for Haughley to become a London overspill town with a population of 40–50,000 adjacent to the M45. We have to be grateful that 40 years later we live in what is still a pastoral landscape.

The Post Mill with Sam Goode on the steps, c.1925.

Chapter Eight

Local Characters and Their Stories

David Fleetwood and Geoff Clarke

English village communities, with their wealth of history, are bound over the years to have seen countless local characters. Haughley is, of course, no exception. It has been immensely enjoyable researching this chapter, scouring the archives, surfing the net and, most importantly, talking with Haughley villagers. Clearly, no book would be large enough to include information on all the many characters who, over the years, have been born, grown up, and spent their working lives in the village. The challenge, then, has been who to include! In rising to this challenge we have decided to focus on characters of the twentieth century, and have aimed to include characters from a variety of walks of life, ranging from those who have justly been considered locally to be the 'salt of the earth', but of which little is known outside of Haughley, to those who have achieved national and international acclaim for their work.

George Clements

There have been many local characters who can justly wear the 'salt of the earth' tag, and have typically worked hard all their lives for the benefit of the Haughley community. One such character was George Clements. Born in 1898, George lived all his life in Haughley. In his retirement George reflected on his early life and we are fortunate that some of his stories have been captured on audio tape. The stories below are transcripts from those recordings, and give some insight into the life of a schoolboy in the early 1900s:

The Broken Lamp Glass

When I went to school I can remember three of us, Sam Hunt, Donny Moss and me pitching our hats up in the girls' place, and of course down came the lamp glass, and of course when he come back, I can see him now hitting his old leg. The girls said 'Please Sir, George Clements, Sam Hunt and Donny Moss have been throwing their caps and they've broken the lamp glass in our cloakroom.' Well of course we came out – I was never caned so much in all me life. We sat and cried all afternoon, we couldn't use that hand where he thrashed us, and he said you can all bring three halfpence, a penny halfpenny each tomorrow morning to my desk, and he gave us all a halfpenny each back. They used to be four pence halfpenny, a lamp glass at that time.

Pigs' Bellies

I used to take home pigs' bellies in a pail, and do you know what, they used to scrape them and get two basins of lard, and then she [his mother] used to cut, not actually the pig's belly, but sort of the outside, she used to cut off and make chiplets and put currants and sultanas with it and put them in a turnover. Oh by God we was bad off.

Waiting for the Twelfth Egg

Miss Lincoln used to teach the older children. Of course when I lived at the bottom of the lane I used to bring eggs to Mash's shop, a dozen, and take them back in grosses. Well that Miss Lincoln used to teach us. I'd got eleven eggs but I'd got to wait until the hen had laid the twelfth. Every time that character went up the yard and they'd have a look and say 'no he hasn't laid.' I said 'I can't wait much longer.' Well I went in school that day – they'd mark the register about quarter to ten – I should think it was quarter past ten, and do you know that there Miss Lincoln couldn't cane me for laughing. She said 'why are you this late?' I said 'well I had to wait until the hen had done laying.' Well she said 'How did you know the hen was going to lay laying?' I said 'Well it was sitting on the nest and I said my mother wanted to make it up to a dozen eggs 'cos I'd got to take the equivalent grosses back when I was coming home from school.' She was a'laughing so much she couldn't cane me.

Jimmy Mulley

Jimmy was a kind and generous man who gave freely of his time to help and support others in the village. Born in 1905, he enjoyed country life to the full, and remained active until shortly before his death in 1997. Indeed, in his latter years he was often still to be seen forking horse manure into sacks for the garden, and on one occasion, at an age when most people prefer to relax and let others do the work for them, was spotted clambering up a ladder to make some repairs to the roof of his cottage. For many years he regularly followed the Suffolk Hunt, on which occasions he was often to be seen wearing a hard hat and carrying an umbrella. He particularly enjoyed a traditional glass of port at these Hunt meetings, and was said to have been disappointed on one occasion when he arrived to find the port had all gone! Marion McPherson is one of many

Jimmy Mulley, 1996. (PHOTOGRAPH GEOFF CLARKE)

Haughley villagers who have fond memories of Jimmy:

Having known Jim Mulley ever since I was a small girl, to this day I can close my eyes and almost see him riding his bike down the village street, zigzagging from side to side, whistling or singing at the top of his voice. Both of my grown-up sons also have fond memories of Uncle Jim. He was known as this because of his wife's connection with my mother's side of the family. They were second cousins.

As little boys, they loved Uncle Jim's strange, somewhat childish, antics and the seemingly never-ending supply of sweets that issued forth from his coat pocket, making him a firm favourite in their eyes. Sadly, Jim never had any children of his own but he would have made an ideal grandfather. Later, as they grew into their teens, my sons still loved to visit the Mulley household whenever they came over to England from America on holiday. On one particular occasion when my son was age 14, we went over to their cottage for a visit. I was offered a sherry and my son a glass of lemonade. Whilst Aunt Nora was in the kitchen preparing the drinks, Jim nudged my son and gave a wicked wink. 'The wife doesn't know it but I've got some really good stuff (meaning hard liquor) up the shed.' Apparently, Jim spent quite a lot of time up at that old garden shed. On another occasion, my eldest son was spending time in Haughley, and being an 18-year-old, got a little restless. Being a kind-hearted chap, Jim offered to take my son to Bury St Edmunds for an afternoon. Thinking that Scott would enjoy a chance to see the beautiful English countryside, they took the longer, more scenic route, meandering their way through various off-the-beaten-track villages and overgrown narrow lanes. It took about two hours to reach Bury. Later that evening when I spoke to my son on the telephone he told me he had been quite petrified by Jim's driving. It wasn't speed or recklessness but the fact that he continually kept pointing out places and things of interest, and consequently veering across the road and mounting the verges.

We all suspected Jim was a little hen-pecked but in many ways he was his own man, never quite conforming to what a respected schoolteacher's husband should be or behave like. Many was the time he caused his dear wife to cringe with embarrassment. My mother related one such story to me that took place in a rather posh teashop at a 'select' seaside resort. Dropping his wife and the two friends off, Jim went to find a parking space. Aunt Nora suggested they go in and find themselves a table and wait for Jim. After a lapse of some ten minutes or so, Jim finally entered the establishment and literally danced his way across the floor, yodelling and swinging his walking stick on route to their table. He appeared totally oblivious to the disapproving looks of the other customers and of course, his wife's glare.

Jim was a notorious scavenger. Aunt Nora would constantly throw things out only to have them stealthily retrieved by Jim and stashed in the garden shed. He was also known to raid skips whenever anything interesting caught his eye. He was a firm believer in the daily walk and this was often a good excuse to retrieve useful and useless stuff. If he found something which he considered to be of value and might like to be recovered by the owner, he would take the item down to the police station. Of course, each visit meant a report had to be filed, questions asked, etc, and after numerous trips he became quite well known and regarded as 'a bit of a nuisance'. The police constable on duty usually gave a groan whenever they saw Jim approaching the desk, 'a find' in hand.

After the death of his wife, Jim became a bit of a hippie, sporting a long beard and wearing old clothes that were past their best. One afternoon my mother took over a plate of home-baked goods and was quite

Jimmy Mulley, in a portrait taken in 1993. (PHOTOGRAPH GEOFF CLARKE)

LOCAL CHARACTERS AND THEIR STORIES

shocked to find that the once-highly-polished sideboard in the front room was being utilised as a tool bench. Where the china and knick-knacks once stood, there was now a row of hammers, wrenches and spanners.

Jim loved the sporting life and went shooting and followed the hounds (by car) at every opportunity. He would often roam the meadows of Dial Farm with his shotgun. Luckily for Jim these meadows were sandwiched between two of Mr Bevan's properties, both well stocked with pheasants. I was told that after Jim became a widower he no longer went to the shed to pluck and dress his birds but did the same in front of the living-room fire. Surrounded by piles of feathers and down, had a spark flown out, it could have proved quite a dangerous situation, but then Jim did like to live a little dangerously as we all know, climbing tall ladders and the likes.

Harry Pryke

No chapter on characters would be complete without a mention of Harry Pryke. Over the years Harry had a variety of roles in the village including taxi driver, hairdresser, and ARP warden during the Second World War. However, Harry will be best remembered as the local harness maker. In this capacity, Harry became well acquainted with, and fond of, a horse named Tishy. Following Tishy's 'retirement' her head was proudly displayed in Harry's front window. And that, so people thought, was that! But people 'thought wrong', as Tishy was to have a new lease of life. Anecdotal evidence suggests that in 1935, during the celebrations of the silver jubilee of King George V, Tishy was once again seen plodding the streets of Haughley. Indeed, she was seen on many occasions thereafter, and in particular took her place in carnival processions through the village.

In 1944 Tishy played her part in raising money for the 'Welcome Home Fund' (see page 140). She was led round the village by Harry who donned a false moustache for the occasion, and kept her under control by brandishing a horsewhip. Local villager

Wedding picture of John Aldous and Hilda Pryke, with Harry 'Waxam' Pryke to the right of the bride, in 1935.

Jimmy Mulley enjoying a singsong with Sarah Clarke at the piano in 1993. (PHOTOGRAPH GEOFF CLARKE)

Dennis Spink remembers Tishy rearing up when frightened by a passing Eastern Counties bus that sounded its horn. Dennis also remembers that, in order to provide an extra touch of realism, Tishy's 'rear person' would be equipped with a bag of chocolate buns that would be dropped at strategic intervals along the street.

Roy Palmer

Haughley is well known for many things, not least for the excellent Palmer's Bakery, established by William James Palmer back in 1869. The bakery is located on the site of the old market stalls on the village green, and it was in the actual bakery building that, on 9 June 1918, Roy Palmer came into this world, son of William Ewart Gladstone Palmer and his wife Mabel Florence Palmer (née Woods). Roy and his brothers Eric (known as Tom) and Ronnie were brought up by a nanny, Maud Lord, who was absolutely devoted to the boys. The boys all belonged to the Boys' Brigade, and one of the highlights for them was the annual camp at Hemsby, paid for by their father. Roy was not conscripted into the Army, he joined before the Second World War started, and went on to serve in Northern Ireland, Egypt, Palestine, France and the Shetland Isles. It was whilst stationed on the

Margaret and Roy Palmer in the 1980s.

Cherbourg peninsula, France, that Roy had a narrow escape. German tanks were approaching and Roy, together with others in his unit, retreated to the coast. With the Germans fast closing in they managed to find and commandeer a fishing vessel, in which they sailed back across the Channel to safety. On a lighter note, Roy used to recall his experiences in the Royal Army Service Corps in the Shetland Isles, and in particular would tell the story about mice falling into the dough bowls in the bakery, thereby adding some unintended flavour to the bread – it should be emphasised that this practice has never been adopted at the Haughley bakery!

Roy Palmer displays an ancient 'True terrier' (an inventory of items in a building).

It was in 1942, whilst serving in Northern Ireland, that Roy met Margaret, a member of the Women's Auxiliary Corps. Margaret was busy serving and mistakenly tried to charge Roy for his first drink (it was normal practice for the first drink to be free). This got them talking – a whirlwind romance followed, and they were married in 1943. They had two children, Kenneth born in 1945, and Gordon born in 1950. After the war Roy's father decided to take semi-retirement and set about delegating to his sons: it was agreed that Eric would run the mill, farm and piggeries; Ronnie would run the insurance business; and Roy would run the bakery, and in addition would look after the estate and property business.

Roy had many interests outside of work – before the war he had been a keen footballer and played left back for Haughley United; after the war he was for several years chairman of the Village Hall Reading Room, and was president of Haughley Bowls Club. He was an Ipswich Town shareholder, and used to tell the story of how, on a particularly hectic day, he was driving to a shareholders' meeting and realised, as he approached Ipswich that he was still wearing his carpet slippers. Undeterred, Roy stopped off at Coes Men's Outfitters and bought himself a new pair of shoes for the occasion! Roy also took a keen interest in local history, and following an exhibition in 1973 to commemorate the 900th anniversary of the destruction of Haughley Castle, founded the Haughley Bakery Museum, believed to have been the only museum of its type in the United Kingdom, and one of only three in Europe. It is estimated that approximately 1,000 groups were given guided tours of the museum between 1973 and 1988, and the income from visitors enabled over £10,000 to be raised for the Bakers' Benevolent Fund.

Roy died on 14 December 1989, but the Palmer heritage in Haughley survives and continues to flourish, through Roy's son Ken and his wife Christine, and Roy's grandson, Kieron.

Alfred Woods

Alfred Woods was one of the great Haughley characters of the late-nineteenth and early-twentieth centuries. The son of Charles Woods and his wife Elizabeth Woods (née Andrews), Alfred (full name Ephraim John Alfred) was born in Haughley on 23 November 1864. He was brought up in the village, and on 1 November 1882 married Rosina Rye whose father, Samuel, was the local rake maker. Alfred and Rosina had one daughter, Mabel Florence (who was to marry William Ewart Gladstone Palmer and was mother of Roy Palmer whose life is described above).

During Alfred's early adult life he worked for a period at the Foreign Office, then in due course he inherited the Haughley coach-building business from his maternal grandfather, William Andrews. Alfred and his brother Edgar (full name Henry Charles

LOCAL CHARACTERS AND THEIR STORIES

Three generations of the Palmer family, the village bakers, c.1985. Left to right: *Kieron, Roy and Ken.*

Edgar) ran the coach-building business for many years, but Alfred had much business acumen and an entrepreneurial streak: he also owned and managed Green and Mill Farms, and was extremely active in the local property market, establishing a reputation as a benevolent landlord.

In addition to his business interests, Alfred was involved in all sorts of other aspects of Haughley village life: he was the village postmaster for 35 years; he was the first chairman of the Parish Council; he was a Haughley Crawford's School governor; he was a parish warden; he was a churchwarden of St Mary's, Haughley, for approximately 30 years; he was secretary of the Haughley and Wetherden Conservative Association; he was for many years one of the main organisers of the annual fête and flower show; he was vice-president of the Reading Room; he maintained records of local history; he was honorary treasurer of the Haughley, Wetherden and Harleston District Nursing Association; and was also a trustee of the Parish Poor and Coal Charities.

When Alfred died in 1931, Haughley lost someone who during his life had justly earned a reputation as a pillar of the community.

Mr Alfred Woods, c.1925.

Revd Walter Grainge White

Revd Walter Grainge White became vicar of Haughley in 1921, and throughout his ministry in the village was fully committed not only to his pastoral duties, but also to the improvement of the local living conditions. A colourful character, he was a man with an inquiring mind, full of curiosity, and was also a man of principle who worked unceasingly for the benefit of his flock. His doggedness in pursuing causes in which he believed meant that from time to time he became involved in public disagreements, but his 35-year tenure as vicar of the parish is testimony to the general high regard with which he was held.

Born in British Guiana (now Guyana), Revd Grainge White was ordained in 1906. From 1908 to 1913 he was chaplain to the governor of Burma, and founded and taught in a school at Moulmein. From 1913 to 1915 he was a missionary to the Makuchi Indians on the Rupununi River, and then in 1916 he became the acting chaplain at HM Penal Settlement in British Guiana. He took a great interest in geographical studies, and in 1915 became a fellow of the Royal Geographic Society. His interest in the people of the world was again in evidence in 1922 when he wrote, and had published, a book entitled *The Sea Gypsies of Malaya,* an account of the Nomadic Mawken people, inhabitants of the islands off the Burmese/Thai coast.

Appointed vicar of Haughley in 1921, Revd Grainge White set about his 'missionary' work in the parish. He set out not only to look after his parish's spiritual needs, but also its social well-being. He was one of the prime instigators for council-housing to be provided in the village, and famously, in the early 1930s he battled on behalf of his parishioners to improve the dreadful problems resulting from the lack of a proper sewerage system. His unstinting efforts to make improvements became widely known as a result of which an article was printed in the *News of the World* under the headline 'The Death-trap Village'. The following is an extract from that article:

For the past five years the local vicar, the Rev W G White, has been engaged on a long and almost hopeless battle with the apathy of the district council to secure improved conditions for his unfortunate parishioners. On two occasions he has brought actions for libel and secured damages, once in open court. Petty local government politics have ruined practically every effort. Shortly after his arrival in the parish, and despairing of making any breach in the dead wall of opposition, he allowed himself to be sued for rates to bring the matter into the open. So far almost the net result of all this endeavour has been the provision of a cart by the district council to remove the privy middens, which previously had to be buried in the tenants' yards! A few houses have been built recently, which have done little to obviate the terrible overcrowding

John Howson recording a song by Ted Chaplin in the old back bar of the King's Arms in 1989.

The Ron Crascall Pavilion, named in honour of Ron Crascall who made a major contribution to village life. In his time he was a great sportsman, parish councillor, district councillor, county councillor and JP.

❖ LOCAL CHARACTERS AND THEIR STORIES ❖

Mrs Alice Parker does the washing, c.1950.

Above: *Ron Crascall, c.1980.*

Right: *Hammond Taylor in typical organising mode.*

which exists in the village. There are still cases of eleven people occupying a small cottage with one bedroom, ten in a cottage with two bedrooms, eight in a cottage with one bedroom, and a landing used as a bedroom. From almost every house channels flow into an open sewer along the street conveying liquid sewage. Children fall over into this mess. The channels are swept once a week and become frequently choked. In hot weather conditions are ghastly. A system of piping was proposed five years ago. The original scheme would have cost less than £300 and added hardly anything to the local rates, which would be chiefly borne by influential local inhabitants.

A smartly dressed, dapper man, Revd Grainge White was often to be seen riding his bicycle around the village. He was passionate about village matters, became a parish councillor and was also elected to the District Council. He was an accomplished musician and enjoyed flourishing the baton when conducting the choir at Thursday evening rehearsals. He also played the piano and regularly played at church concerts. He was also a keen ornithologist, which no doubt explains why the monthly *Parish Newsletter* was, during the 1930s, entitled *A Little Bird*. The interest in birds was again in evidence in 1942 when letters were published in the *East Anglian Daily Times* regarding the first sightings of birds in the spring. Revd Grainge White was apparently the first to see a chiff chaff, on 7 April in Abbey Gardens, Bury St Edmunds, and the first to see a nightingale, on 14 April in Haughley.

During the war years, when American soldiers were stationed around Haughley, Revd Grainge White believed that his early life in Guyana meant that he was well qualified to entertain the black troops. On 23 September he wrote the following letter, published in the *East Anglian Daily Times*:

I should like it to be known that Mrs White and I will welcome visits from Negro or coloured troops, to whom Haughley is accessible. The Vicarage Rest Room – so long as we can afford to keep it open – will be for their use. It has comfortable furniture, writing table, and free materials, papers and books, a wireless and a good piano. As I was born in Guyana and attended the Grammar School, mixing with boys of different races, and as I travelled to the Guyana diamond fields and worked there with a Negro friend, and Negro and coloured men, visitors may feel assured that our welcome will in no way be tainted with condescension.

Revd Grainge White's 'open door' policy was also evidenced when he regularly allowed German prisoners of war into the Vicarage to use the bath. His generosity was not always returned, and he was on one occasion 'shopped' for allowing the lights in the church to be on during the blackout!

In terms of theological matters, one of Revd Grainge White's claims to fame was that he disagreed

Revd and Mrs Grainge White taking tea in the Village Hall.

with the usual wording of the Lord's Prayer, and wrote his own version for use in church services in Haughley. His version was used in Haughley church services from 1929, and in May 1956 his book entitled *Annotated Analysis of the Christian Family Prayer* was published.

Mention must be made of Elisabeth, Revd Grainge White's wife, who quietly supported him throughout his ministry. Elisabeth ran the Sunday school, the Mothers' Union and the Girls' Friendly Society, and also brought up their five children!

Revd Walter Grainge White retired in 1957 after devoting 35 years of his life to the village of Haughley.

Lady Eve Balfour

Lady Eve Balfour was a truly remarkable person. She is best remembered as being a pioneer of organic farming and being the founder member of the Soil Association, but that was never to the exclusion of other pursuits. She was also an accomplished

Lady Eve Balfour, a founder of the Soil Association and inspiration for the organic farming movement.

musician, at one time playing the saxophone in a dance band that performed in the White Horse in Ipswich. She was a writer of some merit, co-authoring three detective novels. In addition she was an experienced sailor and a qualified pilot. She was born on 16 July 1898 into a family of some renown: her father, Gerald Balfour, was chief secretary for Ireland, and her uncle, A.J. Balfour was a prime minister.

Lady Eve studied at Reading University where she gained a diploma in Agriculture. When only 21 she bought New Bells Farm in Haughley Green. From the outset she showed herself to be a young woman of courage and principle, prepared to stand up for and support causes in which she believed. Her gritty determination was certainly in evidence during the 'Tithe Wars' of the 1930s. As Fred Stilwell reflects in his book *Lady Eve, Haughley & The Soil Association*:

Tithes were an ancient practice whereby a levy was made by the Church upon the crops. In 1936 the tithe had been fixed at one tenth of the value of certain crops, but with the fall in prices this charge fell harshly upon the farming community. Many could not pay the tithe and as a result bailiffs would be sent in to claim goods in lieu of payment. Farmers banded together and systems were set up to warn of bailiffs in the district. Often fights would break out as farmers tried to protect their property. Lady Eve was to the fore of such protests. Lady Eve was summonsed, but her plea, supported by her pamphlets, won the day and doubtless helped to bring about a solution. In 1936 the Government paid compensation to the Church, and took over the tithes. Over the following years a redemption charge was levied upon all the lands involved and the system was thus extinguished.

Throughout the 1930s Lady Eve became increasingly critical of trends in farming methods, and in particular the intensification of farming, and decided that research was required to understand better the interrelationship between the soil, plants, animals and man. The subsequent research undertaken at New Bells Farm in the early 1940s became known as 'The Haughley Experiment' – a whole farm dedicated to organic farming research, which lasted for 35 years. By 1943 sufficient research had been undertaken, and Lady Eve published the initial results of the research in a book entitled *The Living Soil*, still recognised as a classic, authoritative source of information on organic matters. Two years later, Lady Eve invited a number of persons prominent in the field to discuss how research from different countries of the world should be brought together and further work co-ordinated. From this meeting the idea of a Soil Association was conceived, and in May 1946 the inaugural meeting of the Soil Association took place.

Lady Eve's reputation as a pioneer became known worldwide, and she spent considerable time travelling the world, lecturing and promoting the aims of the Association. By the end of 1948 the Association had 2,000 members spread across 32 countries. Research work continued, despite various funding difficulties over the following decades, and in 1975 the findings of the Haughley Experiment were updated and republished by Lady Eve.

In her later years, Lady Eve was gratified to see the growth in interest in organic agriculture. Her contribution to the organic movement was recognised by her appointment as OBE, just weeks before she died in 1990, aged 91. Throughout her life, Lady Eve was committed to vegetarianism and healthy eating. However, on her own admission she did from time to time indulge – she was once asked to address a group of serious-minded people about healthy nutrition. During this address she was asked her about her own diet. 'Oh, don't model yourself on me', she replied. 'I drink gin and tonic and smoke cigarettes. As long as you're good 75 per cent of the time, the remaining 25 per cent will look after itself.'

Richard Coe and other village museum pieces.

ESTABLISHED 1904

SPECIALISTS IN HIGH CLASS JOINERY, PANELLING
AND INTERIOR DECORATIONS IN WOOD

JOINERY WORKS
STOWMARKET

YOUR REF.................   OUR REF. CGW/BRB.

Mrs. K.A. Coe,   16th. August, 1961.
Old Street,
Haughley,
Nr. Stowmarket,
Suffolk.

Dear Madam,

    I thank you for your letter of the 12th. instant, and am pleased to note that your son Richard is anxious to become a carpenter.

    I also note that he is leaving school at the end of the year, and in the meantime I would be pleased if he called at my office for an interview.

    Perhaps you will notify me of his intended visit.

Yours faithfully,
for THE STOWMARKET TIMBER Co. LTD.,

C.G. Whiting.
Director.

Above: *Richard Coe is summoned for interview.*

A portrait of Sam James.

Richard Coe and Robert Stiff square up the village pump.

LOCAL CHARACTERS AND THEIR STORIES

Bacton School rock band, 'The Undiscovered', at the Encore Theatre Group variety show in 1993. Left to right: Adam Colthorpe, Christopher Last, Cindy Coshall, Rebecca Froude, Kate Hefferman, Katie Krykant.

Harry Pryke 'supervises' riding at a Plashwood fête in the 1930s.

Haughley cricket team, winners of the Walsham and District League in 1952. Left to right, back row: B. Armstrong, J. Denny, D. Thompson, D. Duncan, E. Duncan, J. Howard, J. Dearsley; front row: J. Buss (?), J. Pulton, J. Turner (president), D. Keenan (captain), Mr A.W. Matthews (hon. sec.), P. Cook, J. Burman (umpire).

Ida Witherley presents a cake to John Prigg on his retirement in August 1992. Ida was John Prigg's first and last customer in his Haughley butcher's shop.

Chapter Nine

Village Organisations and Celebrations

Celia Stephens

Organisations

The last quarter of the nineteenth century saw the growth of the kind of village organisations that still flourish in 2005. In 1854 common land at Haughley Green was set apart as a recreation-ground, which became known as 'The Cricket'. *White's Directory* of Suffolk from 1855 mentions a 'fair for toys, pleasure, etc is held on 26th August each year.' Other sources report that the fair was held on the 15th, which is the Feast of the Assumption of the Blessed Virgin Mary – a fair to coincide with the dedication of the Parish Church seems more likely. The toys would have been cheap trinkets or 'fairings' and there would have been peddlers (so not so very different from our modern street fairs!). Unfortunately, the people entered into the spirit of the occasion too much, and as a result of riotous behaviour fairs fell into disrepute. Haughley's, along with other local fairs, was stopped following an Act of Parliament in 1871.

In *Haughley Past and Present* Nigel MacCulloch provides a portrait of parish life, gleaned from the *Parish Magazines* of 1875–76. Sport was already a feature – there was a thriving cricket team, a quoits club and the beginnings of a football side. On Easter Monday in 1875 the cricket club organised a sports meeting followed by a parish tea. Colonel Walter Tyrell, who lived at Plashwood, presented the prizes which included 'a plum pudding, a water pot, a rake, a tea and coffee pot, a hoe, three jugs, a zinc pail, a comb and brush set, a loin of pork, a pound of tea, 20 eggs, a pair of chickens, a cock and hen' – all very practical at a time of low wages. There is also information about church activities, such as a Sunday school treat at Haughley House and a choir outing to Harwich. There were talks – not surprisingly many were about missionary work and charitable activities. However, a public library and the Reading Room were set up at this time and the directors also organised lectures and concerts. Mention is made of a lantern

Haughley Cricket Club, 1911. Left to right, standing: C. James, Herbert Andrews, Jim Pawsey, William Felgate, Chas Pollard, Chas Elmer, Jack James, Henry Cornish (schoolmaster), Bob Adams; sitting: Herman Denny, Walter Denny, Ernest Felgate, William Drake.

A musical entertainment in the Village Hall during the 1950s.

A celebration in the Village Hall, c.1951. The picture includes: Mrs Rice, Mrs Ling, Mrs Moss, Dora Pryke, Peggy Reynolds and her mother-in-law, Mrs MacCulloch, Ida Witherley, Nellie Rushbrook, Zena Bullett, Mrs Sillett, Ivy Edwards, Eva Murton.

VILLAGE ORGANISATIONS AND CELEBRATIONS

A celebration in the Village Hall, 1930s.

A Christmas dinner in the Village Hall, 18 December 1951. The picture includes:'Bar We' James and Mrs Cutting.

lecture (an early kind of slide show) illustrating a 'Tour of India' and the Choir of St John's Church, Bury St Edmunds, came to give a concert which was a sell out with 250 present.

The twentieth century saw a growth in the number of clubs and facilities for the village. By 1905 the Parish Council had decided that Haughley needed a Village Hall. 'The Cricket' at Haughley Green had fallen into disuse and for some years had been rented out as pasture, from which £191.14s.9d. had been accumulated. It was decided that the former malting on the Folly would be bought and converted for the use of the parish. Mr Wilfred Bevan of Plashwood generously contributed the balance of money required and the new Village Hall was opened by him on Tuesday 17 December 1907. It was reported in *Stowmarket Weekly Post* that 'a large gathering of parishioners assembled' and that 'Master Thomas Bevan unveiled the commemoration stone' – 'Mr Bevan unlocked the doors and declared the building open.' The company proceeded into the Hall and Mr A. (Alfred) Woods, on behalf of the Parish Council, presented Mr Bevan with an illuminated address. Mr Ward Harrison proposed a vote of thanks to Mr Bevan this was seconded by Mr Wenham of Haughley House who:

> *... in an able and encouraging speech pointed out that if such an institution was properly managed, it would result in the social moral and religious well-being of the inhabitants.*

Three hearty cheers were given and the proceeding terminated by the schoolchildren singing the National Anthem.

Over the succeeding decades, village organisations grew and flourished and the hall proved to be a very 'useful place', which is still well used in 2005. Over the years it has been at the centre of village gatherings, suppers, exhibitions, sales and events. In the 1970s it became the home of Haughley Pre-School and the Pit Stop after-school club was formed in 2003.

It has also been the setting for drama productions

Alf Stamp and John Nunn acting in A Canterbury Christmas, *a play by Lady Mary Balfour.*

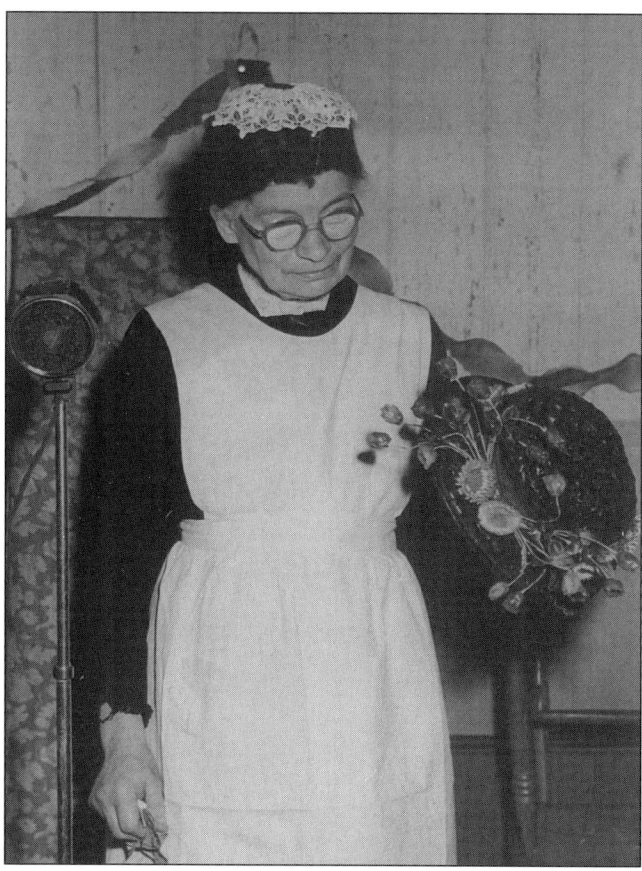

Mrs Grainge White delivers a monologue during a wartime Christmas entertainment.

over the years. During the 1930s Lady Mary Balfour (Lady Eve's elder sister), who was a great enthusiast for amateur dramatics, wrote and produced a number of plays especially for the Women's Institute. Notably, *A Canterbury Christmas* about riots in Canterbury during 1647, which was described in the press reports as 'a great success and exceeded all expectations,' while 'Mr and Mrs J.W. Nunn took their parts in sparkling style as did Miss Kathleen James.' WI productions remained popular events after the war. An initiative to raise money for the Romanian Appeal in December 1989 led to the formation of The Encore Theatre Group. Led by Meg Clarke, this group involved children from four to 18 years of age, and they produced a number successful pantomimes and variety shows.

The Haughley Branch of the Women's Institute was founded in December 1925. For many years it met in the afternoon but meetings were later moved to the evening, providing a welcome night out for the ladies of the parish. As well as drama there was a varied programme of activities – a notable outing was a visit to the House of Commons during the 1950s. The 40th anniversary was celebrated in 1965 and the WI remains an active organisation, about to celebrate its 80th anniversary in 2005.

The origins of the Bowls Club also goes back to at least the 1920s and the enthusiasm of Mr Wilfred Bevan, who presented The Plashwood Cup for an

❖ VILLAGE ORGANISATIONS AND CELEBRATIONS ❖

A production in the Village Hall during the 1950s, starring, left to right: *Mignonette Brunning, Kathleen Coe, Doris Rutherford and Molly Lock.*

A variety show at Haughley, 20 February 1993. For this show The Encore Theatre Group, led by Meg Clarke, joined forces with Richard Leigh, who, with his team, added magic and illusion to the entertainment. Left to right, back row: Lorna Braybrooke, Felicity Herbert, Cheryl Southewood, Richard Leigh, Craig Wallace, Rachel Clarke, Elizabeth Barton, Gemma Langridge; middle row: *Hannah Colthorpe, Kerrianne Smith, Kate Roofe, Rachel King, Carrie Fuller, Tara Bhurakhda, Sarah Langridge, Oliver Betts;* front row: *James Robertson, Elise Pepper, Lisa Jordan, Ruth Bryant, Gemma Clarke, Abigail Nunn (?), Kirsty Smith, Adam Faiers, Ben Kember, Duncan Clark.*

EAST SUFFOLK COUNTY FEDERATION OF WOMEN'S INSTITUTES.

MOTTO FOR THE YEAR 1939.

"Most of the shadows of this life are caused by standing in our own sunshine."

Haughley Women's Institute

COMMITTEE.

President: Mrs. Bevan.
Vice-Presidents: Lady Mary Balfour, Mrs. Brooks and Mrs. Diaper.
Hon. Secretary: Mrs. G. W. Taylor.
Hon. Assistant Secretary: Mrs. James.
Hon. Treasurer: Mrs. Brooks.
Overseas Link Secretary: Miss Debenham.

Mrs. Brunning, Miss Burrows, Mrs. Geatar, Mrs. Knight, Mrs. Jackamen, Mrs. A. Murton, Mrs. G. Robinson, Mrs. Witherley.

SPECIAL DUTIES.

Trading Stall: Mrs. Gladwell and Mrs. Jackamen.

Magazines: Mrs. Aldous.

Press Correspondence and Notice Board: Mrs. James.

Drama Committee: Lady Mary Balfour, Miss Gladwell, Mrs. Knight, Mrs. Nunn, Mrs. Brunning and Mrs. Lock.

PROGRAMME --- 1939.

WEDNESDAY, JANUARY 4th, 2.30 p.m., VILLAGE HALL.
Demonstration: Milk Cookery by Miss Marshall.
Competition: 6 Savoury Sandwiches or 6 Mixed Pastries
Social Half-hour.

WEDNESDAY, FEBRUARY 1st, 2.30, VILLAGE HALL.
Talk on Kenya by Lady Eleanor Cole
Competition: Milk Pudding or Boiled Potatoes.
and Surprise Packets.
Social Half-hour.

WEDNESDAY, MARCH 1st, 2.30, VILLAGE HALL.
Demonstration: Herring Cookery.
Competition: Plain pillow slips or something new from something old.
Social Half-hour.

MARCH — GROUP MEETING in the VILLAGE HALL.

WEDNESDAY, APRIL 5th, 2.30, VILLAGE HALL.
Talk on ...aking.
Competition: ...ads Flour or a bag made from an old felt hat.
Social H...
Rag Col... Hospital.

WEDNESDAY, MAY 3rd, VILLAGE HALL.
Demonstration: Cheap Dinners.
Competition: Cotton Dress not to cost more than 4/-.
Social Half-hour.

JUNE 7th, N.F.W.I. MEETING IN LONDON.

WEDNESDAY, JUNE, 3 p.m., at "PLASHWOOD."
Demonstration: Household Repairs.
Competition: Best home-made article for 1/- or best bunch of garden flowers.

WEDNESDAY, JULY 5th, 3 p.m., at "THE FIRS."
Talk on Making a Newspaper.
Competition: Best bunch of Herbs or Plain Darning.
Social Half-hour.

WEDNESDAY, AUGUST 2nd, 3 p.m., at HILL HOUSE.
Talk: Child Psychology or the uses of canned foods.
Competition: Jar of Pickles or Chutney.
Social Half-hour.

WEDNESDAY, SEPTEMBER 6th, 3, at "NEW BELLS."
Demonstration: Home-made Xmas Gifts.
Competition: Baby's Knitted Coat or Spray of Flowers
Social Half-hour.

WEDNESDAY, OCTOBER 4th, 2.30, VILLAGE HALL.
Demonstration: Cake Making and Icing.
Competition: Blackberry Jelly or Gingerbread.
Social Half-hour.

WEDNESDAY, NOVEMBER 1st, 2.30, VILLAGE HALL.
Demonstration: Paper Flowers.
Competition: Iced Cake or Best Bunch of Autumn Foliage and Berries.
Social half-hour.

NOVEMBER BIRTHDAY PARTY.
Competition: Best Rag Doll or Scrap Book.

WEDNESDAY, DECEMBER 6th, 2, VILLAGE HALL.
Annual Meeting.
Appointment of Tellers and Auditor.
Presentation of Annual Report.
Presentation of Financial Statement for the Year.
Election of Committee by Ballot.
V.C.O.: Address.
Result of Ballot.
Competition: Paper Flowers or best Home-made Loaf of Bread.
Tinfoil for Hospital.

G. R. WILDEN, PRINTER, STOWMARKET.

Haughley Women's Institute programme from 1939.

VILLAGE ORGANISATIONS AND CELEBRATIONS

The 40th anniversary celebrations for Haughley's WI, 1965. Left to right, back row: Pat Soanes, Rosa Sillett, Doris Arbon, Vera Murton, Evelyn Shave, Shirley Coleman, Barbara Steggles, Peggy Reynolds, Gwen Spink; third row includes: Tina Peacock, Dorothy Milner, Ivy Edwards, Ann Marsh, Miss Zena Sillett, Mrs Hall, Kathleen Coe, Mrs Matthews, Joyce Keenan, Eileen Brand; second row includes: Eva Murton, Flo King, Daphne Moss, Mrs Matthews, Dot Arbon, Beryl Jefferies, Ida Witherley, Olive Holland, Mrs MacCulloch; front row: Mrs Jackaman, Mrs Brunning, Mrs Reynolds, Mrs Nellie France, Jean Brand, Enid Thompson, Mrs Hart, Mrs James.

Mr N. Marsh, headmaster Haughley Crawford's School, accepting a cup from Mrs Nellie France to commemorate the golden jubilee of the Federation of Women's Institutes in 1965, which was also the year Haughley WI celebrated its 40th anniversary.

A Haughley WI celebration during the 1950s.

Bob Baldry taking the minutes at a meeting of the joint charities chaired by Mr Dan Harper mid-1950s.

JERUSALEM

And did those feet in ancient time
   Walk upon England's mountains green?
And was the Holy Lamb of God
   On England's pleasant pastures seen?

And did the Countenance Divine
   Shine forth upon our clouded hills?
And was Jerusalem builded here
   Among those dark satanic mills?

Bring me my bow of burning gold!
   Bring me my arrows of desire!
Bring me my spear! O clouds, unfold!
   Bring me my chariot of fire!

I will not cease from mental fight,
   Nor shall my sword sleep in my hand,
Till we have built Jerusalem
   In England's green and pleasant land

—William Blake

K-CARDS — Tel. Billericay 51594
214 Norsey Road, Billericay, Essex

HAUGHLEY WOMEN'S INSTITUTE

PROGRAMME 1987

President: Mrs. A. JONES (673470)

Vice-Presidents:
Mrs. M. COLE and Mrs. D. DUNNINGHAM

Secretary: Mrs. J. RATCLIFFE (673260)

Treasurer: Mrs. P. BURROWS (673381)

Committee:
Mesd. C. Ager, D. Arbon, K. Armstrong, E. Bra[n]
J. Keenan and E. Thompson

Meetings held in the Village Hall on the first Wednesday of each month at 7.15 p.m. unless otherwise stated

---

JANUARY 7th
INDONESIA
With display
Mr. and Mrs. H. Taylor

FEBRUARY 4th
FOOTCARE
Mrs. J. Goldsmith of Scholl Footwear

MARCH 4th
SUFFOLK DEAF AWARENESS SCHEME
With film and talk

APRIL 1st
SPINNING
Mrs. J. Holditch

MAY 6th
RESOLUTIONS
Social evening and Annual Competition

JUNE 3rd
COLOUR ANALYSIS — BEAUTY CONCEPT
Mrs. A. Smith

JULY 1st
OUTING

AUGUST 5th
OUR LOCAL VET
Mr. A. Frackowiak

SEPTEMBER 2nd
FLOWER ARRANGEMENTS
Mrs. F. Phillips

OCTOBER 7th
GLASS ENGRAVING
Mr. S. Oliver

NOVEMBER 4th
ANNUAL GENERAL MEETING

DECEMBER 2nd
BIRTHDAY PARTY

NOTES

Kathleen A Coe
13 Duke Street
Haughley
Stowmarket

The 1987 WI programme.

VILLAGE ORGANISATIONS AND CELEBRATIONS

Harwood Harrison MP with Haughley WI on their visit to the House of Commons in the 1950s.

Haughley Reading Room's quoits team cup winners, 1912–13.

annual tournament organised by Haughley Bowls Club at Plashwood. One newspaper report from the mid-1920s reported that 147 bowls enthusiasts from the surrounding area took part. It was was recorded that, besides the cup, there were gold medals for the winners and silver medals with gold centres for the runners up, handsome walking sticks for the losers in the semi-final, and even the third round got a box of cigarettes. The Haughley Bowls Club green was originally behind the King's Arms, but this was dug up during the war to grow vegetables. In 1946 the club moved to the far side of the King George V Playing Field, where it is at the time of writing. New club facilities were provided in the 1990s as part of the Ron Crascall Pavilion, but members of the Bowls Club funded the addition of a conservatory overlooking the bowls green.

The Reading Room quoits team was also a popular and successful pastime in the late-eighteenth and early-nineteenth centuries.

The opening of the George V Playing Field provided Haughley Cricket Club with a pitch, but there was difficulty maintaining a decent wicket. John Bevan arranged for a concrete wicket which, used with coconut matting, provided a sound surface for bowlers and batsmen alike, and cricket was popular for many years. However, by the 1970s this wicket was no longer serviceable. A grass wicket was relaid but the extension of the football season added to the wear and tear of the ground, making it increasingly difficult to maintain the outfield to a satisfactory or safe standard. After some years of coping with the competing requirements of football and cricket it was decide to wind up the club and the 100-year cricket tradition of Haughley village was brought to a sad end in about 1978. Happily, football continues to thrive. From its slow beginnings in 1875 it has developed into Haughley United Football Club, and has had much success over the years. The club also has a fine clubhouse, which was built in the early 1980s and extended in the 1990s, with the building of the Ron Crascall Pavilion.

In the 1950s there was a popular tennis club, with a grass court where the Scout Hut stands at the time of writing. The Playing Field has a well-used playground for young children, a basketball court and, at the particular request of the youngsters, a skateboard park. Darts and cribbage are still played at the King's Arms public house. The most recently formed sporting club are the Woodwose Archers who have met at Hillcroft School since 2001.

The history of the 1st Wetherden and Haughley Scouts deserves more research, and would most likely result in another book! The Scouts in Haughley started before the First World War and there is evidence to suggest that the 1st Haughley group was in existence within five or so years of Baden Powell's first camp in 1907. 'Barker' Lee was an early member.

During the First World War, N.W. Cutting, a member of the Scout troop, was killed in action, and the troop was present at the dedication of the war memorial in 1920.

Between the wars the troop continued, but records are scarce. However, it is known that they met in the Village Hall. Philip 'Sorter' James was a member and leader during this period and the name was changed to 1st Wetherden and Haughley.

After the Second World War John O. Milner, the District Commissioner for Stowmarket, rescued the troop when the scoutmaster moved away from the village. Instigators of the troop's redevelopment

Bowls winners, c.1950. Left to right: Tom Cutting, Tom Arbon and Bill Robinson.

Above: *Haughley bowls team, c.1950.* The photograph shows: C. Brunning (hon. sec. and treasurer), Mr T. Arbon (captain), Roy Palmer (vice captain), L.F. Whitehead, H. Pryke, A.J. Firman, H. Bowers, J. Strang, C. Green, S. Harper, F. Green, C. Bullett, J. Elmer, E. Quinton, R. Cobbold, 'Dick' Arbon, W. Robinson, A.T. Cutting, L. Arbon. The trophies shown are: the Plashwood Plate, the Stowmarket and District League Cup, the Finborough and District Flower Show Bowls Challenge Cup and the Woolpit Horticultural Show Bowls Challenge Cup.

Left: *Young Woodwose Archers at Hillcroft School.*

Haughley United football team, league champions, 1949. Left to right, back row: Harold Burgess, Tom Ranson, Malcolm Keymer, Jimmy James, Jimmy Ruddick, Donald 'Pedro' James, ? Matthews, Jim Dearsley, Eli Ebenezer Bixby; front row: Charlie Cobbold, Freddy Treehearne, Ivan King, Ronnie James (with cup), Wally Brand, Reg Ager, Fred Sutton. (PHOTOGRAPH ALAN KEYMER)

✦ VILLAGE ORGANISATIONS AND CELEBRATIONS ✦

Scouts at camp in Haughley Park, c.1958. Left to right: Richard Coe, Philip Hart, Gabi Turner, Terry Hearn, Bernard Burgess, Tom Kenworthy (Scoutmaster), Peter Coleman, Geoff Turner, Derek Faiers and Jack Hearn.

Top: *Haughley Scouts camping at Rendlesham Hall in August 1914.*

Above: *'Topping out' the Scout building in the early 1980s. Left to right: David Stiff, Richard Coe, Trevor Stiff, 'Young' Bonnett, Dennis Spink, Maurice Hart, Robert Stiff.*

Richard Coe and Derek Faiers on Scout camp in 1958.

Above, left and right: *1st Wetherden and Haughley Scouts on camp in the early 1950s.*

at this time were John Turner and Mrs Bailey and Mrs Rutherford. The troop became so successful that it built its first Scout Hut, at the bottom of the Playing Field, in the late 1950s. Soon afterwards the Wolf Cub section was formed by Norrie Marsh and Mrs France.

In the early 1980s the HQ was moved to the top of the Playing Field and the Beaver Scout section was formed. The local group is now coeducational and is looking forward to the centenary of the Movement and its own centenary.

Gwen Spink and Ann Hart formed the 1st Haughley Guide Company in 1963. Mrs Betty Palmer of Haughley House presented the company with their Colours, which were dedicated at a church parade in St Mary's Church. They have since flourished, meeting at the Scout Hall and attending many camps. Mary Noy took over as Guider and she went on to become Division Commissioner for Mid-Suffolk. Notable achievements include two Queen's Guides – Linda Davey and Penelope Crease – and, in 1983, Helen Noy was awarded the newly created Baden-Powell Challenge Badge. In the early 1960s the Brownie section was formed with Beryl Jefferies (née Green) as Brown Owl and Marion McPherson (née Balkus) as Tawny Owl. In 1982 the first Rainbow Guide unit in Suffolk opened in Haughley.

The Royal British Legion had an active branch in Haughley, amalgamating with Bacton in 2004, meeting for social activities and to raise money for the work of the Legion. They parade annually for the service at St Mary's Church on Remembrance Sunday, and reinstated the observation of 11 November with a short Act of Remembrance at the war memorial.

The Evergreens meet regularly – there is an active committee, which raises money to pay for a Christmas party and a summer outing, Lowestoft being a favourite destination.

In 1978 the Royal British Legion Sheltered Housing Scheme was opened and various activities are held in the residents' community room. This is known in 2005 as Thompson Court.

A youth club has been active since the Second World War. In April 1967 it was reported in *The Mercury* that the members acquired a solid-oak gate. A team of members, led by Richard Coe, converted the gate into a rustic coffee bar at the club's activity room, at the rear of Haughley Village Hall. It was also reported that the girls were busy making skirts for use by the netball team. Other activities mentioned are visits to the *East Anglian Daily Times*, film shows, football matches and a sausage supper. Entertainment that month was provided by 'Our Generation' and 'The Sonics'. In 1996 Debbie and David Kemp and Jackie Abbott took over as leaders. Known at the time of writing as Haughley Malting Youth Club, the group remains popular and meet in the same clubroom, which is complete with snooker, table tennis and darts facilities. The musical entertainment includes karaoke, while ten-pin bowling and Alton Towers are the kind of outings that are popular with teenagers in 2005.

The Gardening Club meets regularly for talks, demonstrations and outings. For a number of years in the 1980s and '90s Haughley entered the Anglia in Bloom Competition with some success, and people still make a good effort with their hanging baskets and containers.

1st Haughley Girl Guides at the Dedication of Colours Church Parade, 1963. Left to right, in parade order: *Gwen Spink (Guide captain), Olive Burton (assistant commissioner), Sonia Robinson, Jill Faiers, Elizabeth Palmer, Susan Talbot, Rosemary James, Wendy Palmer, Lorraine Joyce, Christine James, Julie Ager, Margaret Laflin, Janet Fisher, Miriam Reditt, Angela Spink, Patricia Keenan, Rae Coe (young leader), Ann Hart (lieutenant).*

VILLAGE ORGANISATIONS AND CELEBRATIONS

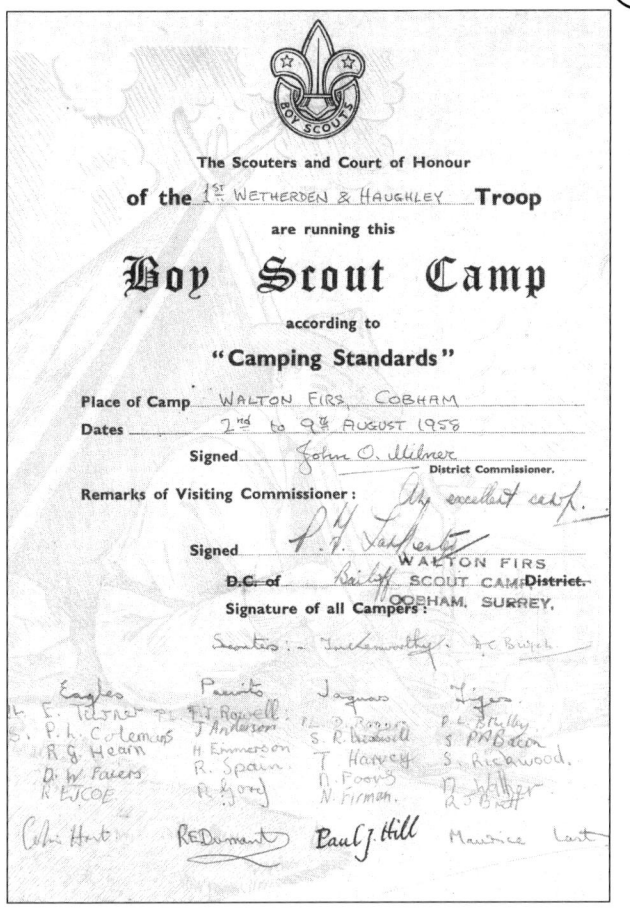

Above: *1st Wetherden and Haughley Scouts at a joint camp with Stowmarket Scouts in 1958.*

Right: *A certificate showing the names of those who attended a Scout Camp at Cobham in Surrey, in 1958.*

Below: *1st Haughley Guides celebrate their first Queen's Guide in 1974. Left to right, back row: Gail Robinson, Jacqueline Knights, Christine Davey, Donna Paddy, Kim Pearmain, Lee Raginbeau, Jane Whomes, Jill Reynolds, Caroline Marschalek; middle row: Judith Parry, Margaret Cobbold, Julie Filby, Fiona McSheehy, Stella Parry, Linda Davey (Queen's Guide), Tracy Harris, Suzanne Hovells, Beverly Laflin, Diane Steggles, Marrion Hovells, front row: Karen Hart, Susan Burrows, Olive Scrivener, Julie Naughton, Melanie Hall.*

Haughley Maltings Youth Club, 2001.

Remembrance Sunday, November 2001.

Left: Revd David Burrell umpires the bowling at Haughley House. The bowlers are John Cattermole, Horry Pryke, Raymond Scott and George Robinson.

A youth club outing to Yarmouth in the 1950s. Left to right, back row: Jennifer Keenan, Carol Pleasance, Shirley Hales, ?, Ken Palmer, Carol Allum, Bobby James, Jennie Bridges, John Faiers, Glynis Talbot, Glynis Hawes, Clive Balham; front row: Reggie Turner, Pippy Faiers, Eric Palmer, Peter Coleman, Marion Balkus, Bill Faiers, Linda Laflin, Margaret Faiers, David Cobbold.

VILLAGE ORGANISATIONS AND CELEBRATIONS

Gardening stall at the Christmas Lighting-up Fayre, being overseen by Rosemary Peck.

The East Suffolk Morris musicians warming up.

Hageneth Morris Men take their title from the old name of Haughley Castle and perform in the village each summer. Not to be outdone, a ladies' dance troop, known as the Haughley Hoofers, was formed in the early 1980s. Both have taken part in street fairs and have travelled extensively over the years.

At the beginning of the twentieth century most residents of Haughley would rarely have left the village, and those who did would not have travelled far afield. However, by the 1980s the UK had joined Europe, so the Haughley and Wetherden Twinning Association was founded to forge links with the village of Noyelle Lèz Seclin, near Lille in France. Each year there is a twinning weekend, alternating in location between Noyelle and Haughley and Wetherden, and many friendships have been made. The Twinning Association run a variety of fund-raising activities to raise money to provide hospitality to the visitors.

Even in these days of television, Haughley residents enjoy making their own amusements. For some time the Haughley and District Gentlemen's Cycling Society, which was formed in 1976, became a regular sight at fêtes and events in Haughley and the surrounding area.

Jeffrey Bowden enjoys his role as lord of the manor and has held occasional manorial courts. Some were held in the King's Arms, which is believed to have been the site of the medieval manorial court. These were enjoyable social occasions and provided a light-hearted atmosphere, in which to discuss any grievances that needed airing. At the time of writing the most recent manorial court was held at Haughley House in 2001, when the 'Freedom of Haughley' was presented to Norman and Margaret Taflinger before their return home to the United States.

No account of village organisations would be complete without mention of our two schools. Haughley Crawford's School, was founded as a church school and is still in use in 2005. It was built at the expense of Mr Crawford of Haughley Park in 1866, at which time families were charged a penny a week for their child's education. The 1875 Education Act brought in free education for all children, but the grant was subject to good reports from a government inspector. Following the first inspection it was recorded by the vicar in the 1875 *Parish Magazine* that 'the boys were well up in arithmetic, weak in notation and their spelling was also weak.' The girls were reported as being 'very weak in arithmetic and the improvement necessary must be substantial.' However, the inspector recommended that the grant should not be withheld and it was hoped that a new mistress would bring an improvement. Mr Cornish was eventually appointed as headmaster, a post he held for 30 years. Headmasters lived in the schoolhouse (now Glebe House) next to the King's Arms – the last to do so was Mr Marsh. The school has been altered several times over the years but the extensions have always been built to blend in with Mr Crawford's original red-brick building. In the 1930s 'The Manual' (now the dining-hall) was added to provide woodwork and domestic science facilities. Originally the toilets would have been outside, but new indoor cloakrooms were added as part of improvements made in the mid-1950s. In 2000 a new extension provided two new classrooms and an activity area.

In the early days children would have spent all their school days at the village school, usually leaving by the age of 15. With the advent of the 11-Plus examination in the early 1960s, pupils changed schools at 11 and went either to Stowmarket Grammar or Bacton County Modern. Since 1978 Haughley Crawford's has only provided primary education and pupils move at nine years of age to Bacton, which is now a middle school, and then on to Stowupland High School.

The history of Hillcroft Preparatory School, now at Haughley Green, can be traced back to the Misses Green's Dame School in Stowmarket. In 1911 this school was taken over by their pupil teacher Miss Hilda Chaplin at the age of 16, and from 1953 the school occupied the seventeenth-century Old Vicarage in Stowmarket. On her retirement in 1961 the school amalgamated with another small school run by June and Gordon Reeder, and continued with great success.

Above: *The Hageneth Morris Men dance outside Antrim House in the 1990s.*

Left: *The Haughley Hoofers at the street fair. Left to right: Juliet Wiles, Glynis Baxter, Jan Butcher, Michelle Francis in Duke Street.*

Sally Taylor, Gill Brett and Jane West lead the Haughley Hoofers at the fair in Duke Street, 1995. (PHOTOGRAPH GEOFF CLARKE)

VILLAGE ORGANISATIONS AND CELEBRATIONS

Haughley and District Gentlemen's Cycling Society, with guest! Colin Hart is enjoying some extra pedal power from Karen Hart, with Alan Noble riding escort.

'Dwoile Flonking' – 'Dwoile' is a Suffolk word for a floor cloth. The object of Dwoile flonking is for the flonker to catch one of the group with a wet dwoile full of beer. If he misses he drinks the beer, if he scores, the loser drinks the beer. A game in which as much beer is spilt as is drunk, but the contestants still seem to get through a few pints!

Haughley Crawford's School netball team, 1959–60. Left to right, back row: Susan Peacock, Sandra Robinson, Cheryl Allum, Margaret Faiers; front row: Glynis Hawes, Gill Brand, Valerie Reason.

In 1981 the headmaster and headmistress, Fred and Gwyn Rapsey, joined the school. Two years later, bursting with pupils, Hillcroft moved to Walnutree Manor at Haughley Green. This gave a dozen acres for expansion and the provision of many specialist facilities. The farmland left by the Soil Association became prepared sports surfaces and many trees were planted. An accredited independent school, its reputation has grown and it continues to feed all the major public schools in Suffolk, maintaining a careful link with state secondary schools – to which it sends about a quarter of its pupils. In 1994 a special unit for dyslexics – the first in East Anglia – was opened. Since 1990 the school has had a 28-bed home in Normandy to which regular study visits take place. The pupils also enjoy taking part in the annual living history event at Kentwell Hall, Long Melford. Hillcroft values its green heritage and, with its links with the Parish Church, St John Ambulance and many other local organisations, is very much a part of the Haughley community.

A strange procession of children celebrating something! Mr Cornish, the headmaster, is directing operations.

Celebrations

The celebration of national events is nothing new and has long been a feature of village life. Then, as now, the church bells would be rung, and records of this exist from as far back as the middle of the seventeenth century. For instance, on 5 November 1664 it was recorded in the Haughley Parish Accounts (held in the Suffolk Record Office) that the ringers were given two shillings for a peal rung to commemorate the deliverance of James I and Parliament from the Gunpowder Plot in 1605. On 23 April 1673 a peal was rung on the anniversary of the coronation of King Charles II, and annually on 29 May, 'Oak Apple Day', to commemorate the Restoration of the Stuarts. Peals were also rung to celebrate the coming of peace as on the 'Reyoycing Day' to celebrate the end of the Anglo-Dutch war in 1674. In 1813 the ringers were given ten shillings for beer on the occasion of the defeat of Napoleon, but were given two pounds for the coronation of George IV in 1821.

Royal jubilees were also celebrated – Thomas Pritty was paid for providing a new clock face and gilt hour hand on the church to commemorate George III's golden jubilee in 1810. On the occasion of Queen Victoria's golden jubilee in 1887 a grand dinner was given for everyone in the parish. Revd MacCulloch recorded in *Haughley Past and Present* that 'Everyone was to share in cold beef, pickles and hot plum puddings, with two pints of beer for each man and one pint for every woman and each child.' The tickets for the dinner guests instructed the 'Bearer to bring plate, knife and fork and pint mug. No Baskets Allowed.' Apparently over 600 people sat down to this meal which was held on the site of the present Village Hall, which at that time was Mr Felgate's malting. This occasion probably also included sports events as there is a record of prizes being given. The overall cost of the celebration was £36.8s.9d. Although the amount of beer consumed in those days has been replaced by the modern preference for wine with meals, the menu is not so very different to what is provided at some village events in the early-twenty-first century, and we still have to remember to bring our cutlery for Harvest Supper.

In July 1919 Peace Day was celebrated to mark the official end of the First World War. A newspaper report tells us that Mr and Mrs Bevan opened the park and gardens at Plashwood and stated that the primary object of the day was to give the children a good time: 'The Children were marshalled at the schools and paraded to Plashwood. There was a programme of sports with an interval for tea. Miss Bevan was kept busy providing music on a gramophone.' (No doubt during this period there would have been a wind-up gramophone.) A bowls match between Plashwood and the village provided entertainment for the adults. In the evening a whist drive and a dance were held for the grown-ups in the Village Hall, which had been vacated by the last batch of German prisoners of war only a few days previously. During the day the Union Jack flew from the church tower, and flags and bunting gave the village a festival appearance. A bonfire was lit on the village green at night.

Between the wars there were regular fêtes, horticultural shows and other gatherings.

In May 1935 the village was again decorated to celebrate George V's silver jubilee, and there was a traditional peal of bells and church service. It was from this celebration that there was the first record of there being a fancy-dress parade, which was described in the press 'as an outstanding feature in an attractive programme'. Lady Evelyn Balfour was one of the judges and remarked that the costumes were so good that they were giving away extra consolation prizes. The first prize for the under-nine-year-olds was won jointly by Peter Paddy and June Burman as Darby and Joan, and Audrey and Sybil Allum as Mickey and Minnie Mouse. The over-nines' prizes went to Nellie Witherley as a Victorian lady, and H. Armstrong as an old man. Dennis Spink won a second place as 'Marmalade' – Dennis remembers that his brother

❖ VILLAGE ORGANISATIONS AND CELEBRATIONS ❖

Haughley Crawford's School, 1959–60. Included in the picture are: Jimmy Brett and Derek Faiers (left desk, facing forward), *Philip Hart* (far right), *Tony France* (centre desk), *Tubby Cattermole* (right), *and Bernard Burgess* (front left).

Visitors to the Haughley Fête on 25 July 1922.

The organising committee at Haughley Fête, 1922.

The forerunner, c.1920, of the Haughley and District Gentlemen's Cycling Society?

VILLAGE ORGANISATIONS AND CELEBRATIONS

A makeshift band marches out of Duke Street, possibly for George V's silver jubilee in 1935.

Doris Oram (née Baldry) in fancy dress for King George V's jubilee in 1935.

made a 'Golden Shred' Golly outfit from bits and pieces. In the adult section pride of place went to Mr Harry Pryke and his two assistants for 'their realistic presentation of a horse with its many pranks and caprices.' (This horse was made from the head normally on display in the harness shop window, known as 'Tishy', which became a familiar feature at village events over the years.) Tea was served to the children in the school and to the adults on a meadow lent by Mr J. Barnes, tenant at Castle Farm. Mrs Wilfred Bevan generously donated a jubilee mug for every child. Canisters of tea for women and tobacco for men were presented to those over 65. Mr Paddy was instrumental in raising a delightful improvised band, which headed a procession around the village; a radiogram also provided music. A huge bonfire was lit at ten o'clock and there were fireworks. There was dancing on the village green until the early hours.

The Second World War years intervened but Haughley remained optimistic that the dark days would end. The Welcome Home Committee, led by Mr Bixby, was set up to provide a fund for a celebration when the troops came home. Fêtes and garden parties were able to resume and spirits were lifted by the Festival of Britain in 1951.

For the coronation of our present Queen, on 2 June 1953, a full programme of festivities was organised in Haughley. Very few people had a television, which for the first time beamed a major royal event around the country – most would have seen the coronation ceremony later at the cinema. The day began at 6.30a.m. with the sounding of 'Reveille' from the top of the church tower by John Chaplin, who had been an army bandsman. The flag was unfurled to the National Anthem and the bells were rung.

Following a service in St Mary's Church the celebrations got underway with the fancy-dress parade. The procession assembled at the postbox on Windgap Lane and proceeded all around the village, led by the Combs Silver Band and accompanied by two Scottish Pipers and 'John Bull'. Coronation day was far from being a fine June day – it was very wet. Doris Oram (née Baldry) remembered that, although it was raining and everyone's costumes got very damp, it didn't stop the parade. As they moved up Old Street the Boy Scouts formed an E II R tableau by lying on the green near Dial Farm; Colin Hart thinks that he and Jim Crane formed the II and consequently didn't see much of the procession go by.

The afternoon continued with children's sports, selections from the band and a musical programme broadcast from the radio. Free refreshments were provided for all parishioners with a tea party for the children. Mrs Bevan presented coronation beakers to all children under five and Lady Eve Balfour presented prizes for the competitions.

In the evening there was a men's fancy-dress pram derby which started in Crawford Avenue, following a challenging course via St Mary's Avenue and Station Road, along Old Street, around the Folly to the finishing post in Green Road. This was followed by a comic football match. The evening entertainment included dancing to the Ace Accordion Band, a campfire on the Playing Field with singing and a firework display. John Bean recalls that because of the weather the singing actually took place in a packed Village Hall with Kathleen Coe at the piano. He was probably feeling aggrieved as he had won the pram derby – the prize for which was eight bottles of 'Coronation Beer', but, as he was still only 15 years old, his Uncle 'Farmer' Whitehead took charge of it!

Harry Pryke and the 'component parts' of Tishy, preparing for the fund-raising towards the 'Welcome Home Fund' in 1944. George Lee (left) was the front of the horse, and John Denny (right) was the rear end.

Harry Pryke leads Tishy into the village as part of the fund-raising effort for the 'Welcome Home Fund' in 1945. Behind him are Kate Bean (left) and Eli Ebenezer Bixby (right).

VILLAGE ORGANISATIONS AND CELEBRATIONS

Pat Burrows (née Matthews) as a fancy-dress contestant at the 1951 Festival of Britain Fête on the Playing Field.

Edgar Granville MP, holding Jennifer Keenan, and Mrs Granville with the fancy-dress contestants in the Festival of Britain Fête in 1951. Among the contestants are Pat Burrows (née Matthews) ('Wot, No Meat') and Judy Thompson (née Keenan) ('1951').

A penny farthing for the coronation procession in 1953. Left to right: Dan King, Kathleen Coe, Harry Rutherford, Philip James, Tony Whitehead, Reg Ager and Michael Murton.

Children's tea party in the Village Hall, c.1945, believed to be an end of war celebration. Left to right, far side of table: Pauline Shave, Margaret Lee, Brenda Ransome, Thelma Green, Betty Nunn, ?, Jim Crane, Barry King, John King, Bernard Morphew; near side of table: Pat Bird, Shirley Malster, Joy Bolton, Ruby Crane, Valerie Cobbold, Cecily Messenger.

VILLAGE ORGANISATIONS AND CELEBRATIONS

The children's fancy-dress parade in Station Road, part of the celebrations for the coronation in 1953. Pippy Faiers leads, dressed as a jockey, followed by Richard Coe (as Sir Walter Raleigh) with Graham Lock on his left. In the background are Helen Brand (sunflower) and Rae Coe (an Elizabethan maid) to her left.

Haughley Tennis Club's carnival float for the 1953 coronation celebrations. Left to right: Lewis Hart, Jeff Armstrong, Ray Brand, Connie Rice, John Bean, Bob Holland (as Lady Godiver), Rosemary Hart, Jean Ling, Zena Sillett, Leslie Witherley.

Preparing for the coronation pram race in 1953. Roy Palmer and Dick Arbon are on the left, and Ag King feeds Gladdy Rolf (the 'baby'), watched by Johnnie Nunn and Kate Bean. Behind are Jack Stirzaker and Ronnie Robinson.

Bixby Avenue celebrates the wedding of Charles and Diana in 1981. Amongst the faces that have been recognised are: Sean Paddy, Hayley James, Joanne Thorpe, George Robinson, Dorothy Robinson, Sonia Robinson, Maxine Allum, Keith Robinson, Dennis Allum, Taf Lewis, Michael Lewis, Dirk Forsdyke, Darren Paddy, Eleanor Thorpe, Wayne Fisher, Dean Martin, Kathy Fisher, Jonathan Lewis, Theresa Lewis, Helene Lewis, Sylvia Cobbold, Rosie Cobbold, Maurice Hart.

The coronation set the pattern for future commemorations. The Queen's silver jubilee celebrations took place on Tuesday 7 June 1977. They were held under the chairmanship of Councillor John Prigg, and a series of fund-raising events were organised throughout the year to fund the event. The afternoon began with a fancy-dress parade from the bus shelter to the Playing Field – there were about 100 entrants and the judges were Dr Lower and Dr Dean. There were also the usual sports and competitions as well as handicraft, white elephant and other stalls. Entertainment included a Punch and Judy show and pony rides. The celebration tea was held in the Village Hall, which was suitably decorated for the occasion. Afterwards, the grand draw took place on the Playing Field with a first prize of £50 (quite a lot of money in 1977). All the children were presented with a jubilee mug to commemorate the occasion.

In 1973, the 800th anniversary of the sacking of Haughley Castle, was commemorated with a village museum weekend, with exhibitions of interesting historical items contributed by members of the community. It was on this occasion that the village sign was unveiled. Throughout the 1970s, '80s and '90s there was a succession of street fairs; some with medieval and Victorian themes, and others coincided with lighting up the Christmas tree on the village green. In this type of event there was an echo of the toy fair with a variety of stalls, street entertainers, bands, a fairground and other attractions, with the Hageneth Morris Men and the Haughley Hoofers often taking part. In 1981 several streets, including Bixby Avenue and St Mary's Avenue, organised a street party to celebrate the royal wedding of Charles and Diana. In 1988 a very successful 'Village at Home' exhibition took place.

In the 1960s the first flower festival was organised by Kathleen Coe, and the idea was revived in the 1980s by the vicar's wife, Mrs Angela Twycross, and Nesta Taylor. The festivals have gone from strength to strength, and since 1980 have been an annual event masterminded by Monica Prigg, attracting visitors from all around Suffolk.

In 1995 the 50th anniversary of VJ Day was celebrated with an excellent weekend of events organised by Anita Burrell and Kieron Palmer.

The Haughley and Wetherden Parish News is produced monthly by a band of volunteers and delivered free to every household, to keep everyone abreast of village activities. The many village organisations have their annual round of fêtes, sales and coffee mornings. In particular much hard work and enthusiasm is put into fund-raising events to maintain our ancient Parish Church.

The Queen's golden jubilee was celebrated in 2002. On Sunday 2 June a 'Golden Jubilee Family Service' was held at St Mary's Church, which included the dedication of the new St George's flag which, with the new flagpole on top of the tower, that had been presented by the Palmer family. The Parish Council gave generous financial backing and also funded a 'Golden Jubilee Village Calendar'. A jubilee working party, led by Sue Lewis and made up of representatives from all the village organisations, arranged festivities for 3 June. During the months of planning there had been concern that the kind of

A sale in the Village Hall in the mid-1980s.

VILLAGE ORGANISATIONS AND CELEBRATIONS

A Victorian street fair in 1989.

The Sealed Knot between performances at a street fair.

Kieron Palmer organises a street fair in the mid-1990s.

The Christmas Fayre in 1999, during which the lights on the village green Christmas tree were switched on.

A concert in the church to celebrate the 50th anniversary of VJ Day. Left to right, back row: Sam Galloway, Revd David Burrell, Fred Rapsey, George Parry, David Fleetwood; middle row: Anita Burrell, Janet Sheldrake, Alison Hunt, Pearl Wade, Meg Clarke, Martin Seymour, Sue Fleetwood, Maggie Galloway; front row: Shirley Robinson, Adam Burrell, Sue O'Keeffe. (PHOTOGRAPH GEOFF CLARKE)

Punch and Judy entertaining at a street fair in the 1980s.

✤ VILLAGE ORGANISATIONS AND CELEBRATIONS ✤

Above: *Choir concert in the church, on the 50th anniversary of VJ Day in 1995. Included in the picture are: Shirley Robinson, Anita Burrell, Janet Sheldrake, Sam Galloway, Revd David Burrell, Pearl Wade, Fred Rapsey, George Parry, David Fleetwood, Meg Clark, Sue Fleetwood, Maggie Galloway, Sue O'Keeffe.* (ALL PHOTOGRAPHS GEOFF CLARKE)

Left: *Tom Palmer, Josephine Gibson and Ken Palmer at the VJ Day anniversary celebrations in 1995.*

The 50th anniversary of VJ Day, with teas being enjoyed on the village green, 1995. Left to right, in the foreground: Dot Edwards, Len Arbon, Fred Edwards.

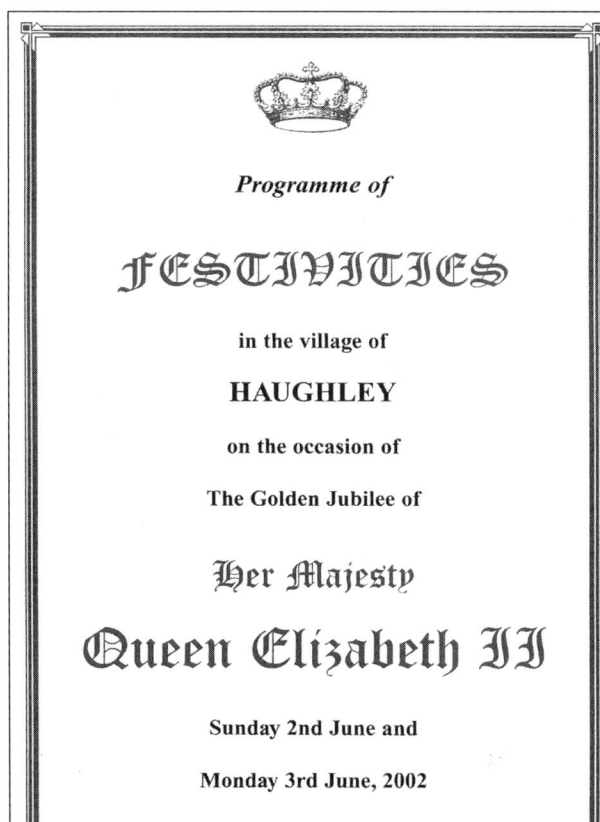

Above: *Philip (Pippy) Faiers – the Eastern Counties light-heavyweight champion in 1966.*

Below: *The Queen's golden jubilee in 2002. Chairman of the Parish Council, Mike Pirrie, presents organiser Sue Lewis with flowers while Jim Crane looks on.*

VILLAGE ORGANISATIONS AND CELEBRATIONS

Norman Taflinger greets guests at Band in the Bailey, 2001. (PHOTOGRAPH GEOFF CLARKE)

Barbara Wallace and Meg Clarke wait for the concert to start in the castle's inner bailey in July 2001. (PHOTOGRAPH GEOFF CLARKE)

Honington Skyliners, under the direction of Dave Charles, prepare to entertain in July 2001. (PHOTOGRAPH GEOFF CLARKE)

VILLAGE ORGANISATIONS AND CELEBRATIONS

Above: *Barry Betts studies his programme with Doreen Stirzaker and Bronwynn Betts looking on at the Band in the Bailey concert, 14 July 2001.* (PHOTOGRAPH GEOFF CLARKE)

Left: *Floodlights were installed at Haughley church to mark the millennium, 1 January 2000.*

traditional day that had worked well in the past might not be so popular in the twenty-first century. The organisers need not have worried. A facsimile of the coronation programme invited parishioners to bring a picnic to the King George V Playing Field for an afternoon of events at the Ron Crascall Pavilion, and the turnout was tremendous.

At 1p.m. the church bells were rung in the time-honoured tradition, and Dave Charles and the Honington Skyliners Big Band entertained. There were some concessions to tradition – instead of fancy dress the children entered a jubilee bonnet parade and 'Dress-a-Bike' competition, and the bouncy castle and face painting were a new addition to the festivities. However, fancy dress was still in evidence in the five-a-side football competition. As well as all the usual activities Geoff Clarke presented an archive film show of 'Haughley Past and Present'. The lord of the manor, Jeffrey Bowden, presented jubilee medals and commemorative mugs to every child in the village. In the evening a barbecue and dance, with the band 'Rifiki', was held in a marquee and the whole village enjoyed Kieron Palmer's spectacular firework display.

For the millennium the Parish Council commissioned a village map, which was given to every household. Floodlighting was installed to light up our beautiful Parish Church, which was switched on during New Year's Eve after a torchlight procession around the village. The new millennium came in to the peal of the church bells and another magnificent pyrotechnic display put on by Kieron Palmer.

'Big Band in the Bailey' was a very special occasion, which took place in 2001. During the 1990s Margaret and Norman Taflinger from Texas were the tenants of Castle Farm House, while they were stationed at Mildenhall Airbase – they quickly became involved in village life. They invited Haughley resident Dave Charles, director of the Skyliners Big Band, to put on a concert of music from the era of Glen Miller. The setting in their garden within the ramparts of Haughley Castle was a natural arena and over 500 people enjoyed an evening of music from the 1930s and '40s.

The year 2000 was a milestone and a time when people naturally looked back on the life and times of the preceding century. As a result the Haughley History Forum came into being to continue recording the recent history of the village. In 2004 a very successful exhibition was put on in the Village Hall to commemorate the 60th anniversary of D Day and life on the Home Front in Haughley during the Second World War. It generated such interest that the group went on to produce this book of memories.

Our thanks to the following for providing information and recollections: James and Alex Bevan for the use of the Plashwood archive; Richard Coe for the use of his archive, Fred Rapsey (more information available at www.hillcroftschool.co.uk); Doris Oram, Colin and Ann Hart, Meg and Geoff Clarke, Nesta Taylor, Gwen and Dennis Spink, John Bean, Sheila Talbot, Sandy McNab, Monica and John Prigg, Sue Lewis and Enid Thompson.

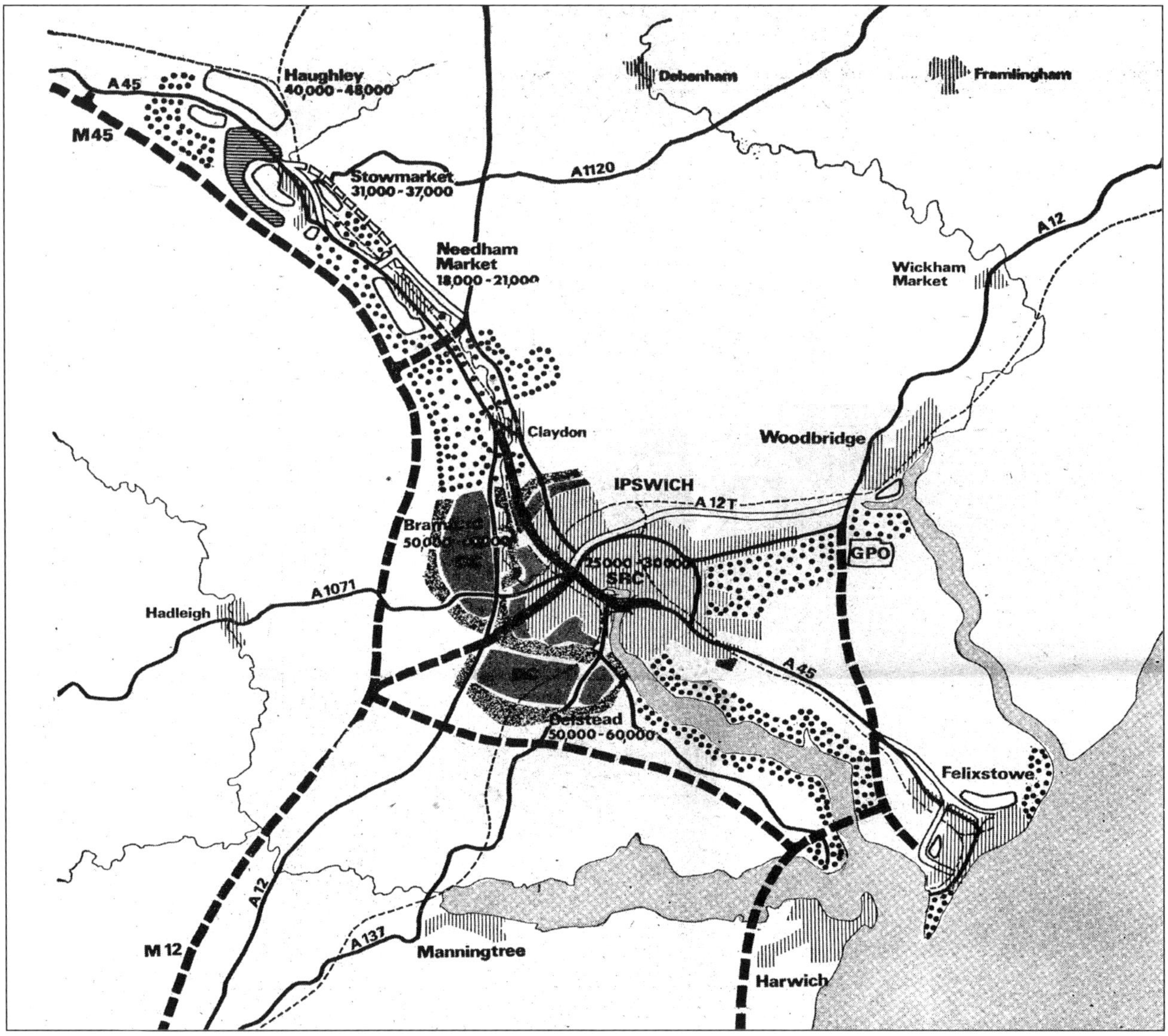

The dream of the 1966 planners for the expansion of Haughley.

An early view of the pump and Rapper Row, remarkably unchanged in 2005, especially now that the modern telephone and electrical wiring has gone underground.

Chapter Ten

Looking to the Future

Howard Stephens

The growth of Haughley has been a gentle journey over the years. From the record of the population in the Domesday Book, through various Pipe Rolls and county directories, it is possible to trace the population and to see that it has increased, but never dramatically. Perhaps the largest single increase was with the building of White City and the houses beyond, which have all come in a relatively short timescale.

In 2005 we can see the steady expansion of the village as gaps between houses are filled and single dwellings and other buildings are pulled down to make way for a number of smaller houses. For all that the population has only doubled over 1,000 years. Some 40 years ago the planners were contemplating the expansion of Ipswich to become a major overflow town for London. It was the idea that greater Ipswich would encompass Felixstowe, Woodbridge, Otley, Haughley, Needham Market, Hadleigh, East Bergholt and Harkstead. Haughley was to be a satellite development of between 40,000 and 48,000 inhabitants and the target date was the year 2000. There is a story from the mid-1960s, when the Ipswich expansion was being considered. Apparently the plan was briefed to the Parish Council but some of the older members of the council found it very difficult to grasp the scale of the new concept: 'Where's 'ey goin' to put all these new howses?' 'On both sides of the main road', explained the visiting planner, 'it will link Haughley and Harleston together into one big settlement.' 'Yoo carn expect folks to walk all that way down from Harleston and over the main rood just to get to p'st office' retorted the councillor, without even dreaming that a population of 45,000 might just need something more than our tiny Post Office.

Fortunately, like George Orwell's *1984* it has not happened, or like *1984* has it? The 'settlement envelopes' have dictated the extent to which the villages and the towns can expand. Nevertheless, as we travel about locally we can see the tentacles of Stowmarket stretching out to wrap around Stowupland and the Creetings. Bury St Edmunds seems to be oozing outwards like an active volcano towards Thurston. The density of dwellings and the inexorable spread of the main settlements mean that over the last 50 years Haughley, like other local villages, is growing at a faster rate than ever before.

There are two paradoxes to this expansion. The first is that the local facilities seem to be diminishing in almost direct proportion to the expansion of population, and the second is that very few of the new dwellings come within the affordable range of those who are born and bred in Haughley. In effect the commuter overspill is starting to happen and, although it is not on the same scale as was envisaged in the plans of 1966, perhaps the predictions were not quite so fanciful as they might have initially seemed.

Of course the proximity of Stowmarket Station with its fast connections to London and Norwich make the area ever more attractive for the commuter but the penalty is that those whose parents' home is here in Haughley, when they come to setting up their own home, have to pay city prices.

Local facilities find it ever harder to compete with the supermarkets and, whilst services are often quite easy to find in and around the village (you only have to look through the advertisements in the *Parish News* to see the range), the basic shopping becomes more and more oriented towards one or other of the supermarkets. We are lucky because we still have the Post Office, the Co-op Shop, Palmer's Bakery, the hairdresser, a vet, the cobbler's and furniture shop, the King's Arms and Maypole pubs, and the Old Counting House Restaurant. To add to the formal outlets there are the front-gate stalls during the year selling eggs, fruit, vegetables, manure, plants, Christmas trees and so forth. If you had to survive without going out of the village you could still feed body and soul. But the trend is worrying and the old adage 'use them or lose them' can never have been truer. Admittedly access and private transport have been revolutionised over the past 100 years, and so getting about is easier and the choice is therefore wider, but over the same period we have lost a dozen shops, at least four pubs, a garage, a forge, workshops, two mills, a chip factory, a butcher's shop, and many local trades with their employment and apprentice

The moat in the snow, 1993. (PHOTOGRAPH GEOFF CLARKE)

The Post Mill, Station Road. The spread of housing over the site makes it difficult to imagine that the mill once stood here, outside the village itself.

LOOKING TO THE FUTURE

opportunities. If this trend is extrapolated in just a few years we shall have nothing, not even an active church or chapel. There will simply be a constant flow of cars taking people to their livelihoods, shopping or leisure.

Mercifully many a Haughley person has enjoyed a long life and several have got very close to or have reached the century. However, on average in 2005 we are all living longer than our predecessors did 100 years ago. The turnover of housing is therefore slower and, even with the new houses coming onto the market, it is always difficult to find a house in Haughley. As we see the price of property today, there will be many a Haughley family thanking their lucky stars that they bought 10, 20 or 30 years ago or more. Even the smallest houses seem to be beyond the reach of the average young family and, unless they are fortunate enough to have significant savings or wealthy and generous parents, it is difficult to see how they can set up a first home in Haughley without a joint income of at least £50,000. Shared equity schemes seem to be the only realistic opportunity for many and these do not often appear. What developers term as 'starter homes' at the planning stage end up as small but expensive pieds à terre for the older and more affluent incomers. This is not a complaint against the new arrivals in the village, for they have their part to play and many now make a highly valued contribution to the village. The result, however, is that the younger adults are driven away to find affordable accommodation elsewhere, the longer established residents are becoming older and the newcomers are people who have already gone a good way through their working lives. We have a gap between them and the teenagers who in just a few years will also be drifting away to find somewhere to live. With fewer young families the school will find it increasingly difficult to survive and the young families we do have will drift off to live nearer a school elsewhere. Will Haughley end up as one vast old peoples' home?

It sounds a gloomy and frighteningly Orwellian prediction of self-destruction. Indeed it could easily be so if we sit back and do nothing. But Haughley folk are not like that, are they?

This is not the place to rehearse answers to all these challenges. But if we are to find the answers then as a community we have to be robust and we have to pull together. We need to work out where we want the village to go and to defend that objective against all-comers. Of course, we cannot possibly all agree with each other on everything; we are bound to have different views and thank heaven for that, but we need to develop the ability, having listened to the arguments, to accept the majority view as to the right path to take.

In putting this book together, the factor that comes through is that as a community we have always had our internal squabbles but when the chips have been down we have pulled together. We have our history and our own miniature heritage of which we can justifiably be proud; we live in an attractive and thoroughly pleasant part of the county; and we may even lose some traffic noise over the next few years! It is also clear from our history that we know how to celebrate and few opportunities have been missed for a good party. As long as we can retain pride in the village, strength and sense of community to defend our way of life, and the sense of fun and humour to enjoy it, then our future is assured. It cannot be achieved without effort but then few things worth having can be.

Facilis descensus Averno; sed ad auras evadere est labor!
(Virgil, Aeneid, V1, 126)

'It is easy to go to Hell;
it's coming back that is difficult!'

A balloon carrying villagers from Haughley sets off towards the sunset, 3 August 1999.

Above: *The village sign and spring blossom in Old Street, 1993.* (PHOTOGRAPH GEOFF CLARKE)

Left: *The Folly in the snow, 1993.* (PHOTOGRAPH GEOFF CLARKE)

Below: *A view of the moat and the Grange, 1993.* (PHOTOGRAPH GEOFF CLARKE)

Subscribers

Connie Ager, Haughley, Suffolk
Patrick D. Ager, Haughley, Suffolk
Owen John Ager, Haughley
Rita Ager, Stowmarket, Suffolk
Mr Bertie Aldous, Haughley
Aubrey C.W. Allum, Haughley, Suffolk
B.J. and S.T. Anderson, Haughley, Suffolk
Gp Capt and Mrs F. Appleyard
Mrs Faith Armstrong, New Street, Haughley
Mr R. and Mrs K. Armstrong, Haughley, Suffolk
Catherine Artindale, Sheffield
Gerard Artindale, Haughley Green
John Artindale, Sheffield
June and Ken Atherton, Castle Rise, Haughley
Mrs B.L. Axten, Kirby Cane
Raymond F. Bailey (Family – Stagg), Newport Pagnell, Buckinghamshire
Tony Baldry, Haughley, Suffolk
Eddie and Sheila Bayfield, Haughley, Suffolk
J.G. Bevan
Mrs Madge Bird, Haughley, Suffolk
Peter R. Bloom, Haughley, Suffolk
Isabel Brand, Old Street, Haughley
Ray and Jean Brand, Haughley Green, Suffolk
Roger Brand, Bury Road, Beyton
Mr Christopher Brett, Haughley, Suffolk
Gill Brett and David Evans, Dial Farmhouse, Haughley
Wendy, Martin, Lauren and Chloe Brinkley, Haughley, Suffolk
Geoffrey and Mavis Brown, Haughley, Suffolk
Zena I.B. Bullett
Rachel A. Buxton, Gislingham, Suffolk
John and Jessie Cattermole, Haughley
Erol E. Clarke, Wetherden, Suffolk
Gemma L. Clarke, Haughley, Suffolk
Meg and Geoff Clarke, Haughley, Suffolk
Thelma Clarke (née Green), Ipswich
Rae M.A. Coe, Witnesham
Richard E.J. Coe, Haughley
Kenneth W. Coleman, Haughley, Suffolk
Ged Cooper, Haughley
Malcolm J. Cooper, Haughley, Suffolk
Mrs B.E. Cornish, Beccles, Suffolk
Lee, Alison, Darryl, Jack Cunnell, Haughley, Suffolk
Trevor J. Davey, Haughley Green, Suffolk
M.G. Davey, Ipswich
S.P. Davey, Haughley
Terry Denny, Haughley, Suffolk
Mrs Jean M. Devenish, Haughley, Suffolk
Brian and Dennis Edwards, Haughley, Suffolk
Raymond L. Edwards, Haughley, Suffolk
Godfrey R. Edwards, Post Office, Haughley
Jean E. Elmer, Haughley Green, Suffolk
Chris Faiers, Haughley, Suffolk
John and Nanette Faiers, Haughley, Suffolk
Philip Faiers, Haughley, Suffolk
Nigel Fellingham, Laurel Farm, Haughley
Robert E. Firman R.M.N., Haughley
Sarah Fitch, Rushden, Northants
David J. Fleetwood, Haughley, Suffolk
Joan E. Fleetwood, Blackmore, Essex
Tony France, Kelvedon, Essex/formerly Haughley
Adrian Frost, Castle Barn, Haughley
Mrs Joan Galois
Julie Garrod (née Naughton), Nettlestead, Suffolk
Ray and Janet Gill, Haughley, Suffolk
Mr and Mrs Gosling, Mutton Hall, Wetherden
Gerald G. Green, Stowmarket, Suffolk
Karen Green (née Hart) and Tony Faiers, Duke Street Haughley
Derrick and Shirley Hall, Haughley, Suffolk
Tony and Rita Hall
Colin and Ann Hart, Duke Street, Haughley
Elaine and Phil Hart, Crowthorne, Berkshire
Maurice Hart, Haughley
Tim and Marike Hart, Millfields, Haughley
Mr Clarence and Mrs Edith Hawes, Haughley, Suffolk
Karl Hawes, Stowmarket, Suffolk
Hombry, Haughley, Suffolk
John and Katie Howson, Haughley, Suffolk
Mr Darren K. Jackson,
Clive Jeffries, Ely, Cambridgeshire
Henry and Beryl Jeffries, Woolpit, Suffolk

Jean B. Keymer, Haughley, Suffolk
Malcolm Keymer, Haughley, Suffolk
Robert S. King
Roy B. King
Mr Philip and Mrs Iris Laflin, Needham Market, Suffolk
Steven Roy Largent, Haughley, Suffolk
George Lee, Haughley. Worked at Palmers Bakery for 52 years
Ian Lewis, Haughley, Suffolk
L.J. Linford, Haughley
Teresa Loveys, Haughley, Suffolk
Anne Marsh, Bexhill, East Sussex
Barry J. Marsh, Widemouth Bay, Cornwall
Ray M. Marsh, Clyro, Hereford
Stephen E. Marsh, Hooe, East Sussex
John, Jo and Sky Marshall, Haughley, Suffolk
Jeremy Matthews, St Erth, Cornwall
Mr and Mrs P. Mayhew, Old Forge, Haughley
Sheila Mayhew, Haughley, Suffolk
A.J. McBain, Claydon, Suffolk
Marion McPherson
Rachel E. Miles, Ipswich
Roger J. Miles
Ruby Ann Millar, Haughley
Julie Minns, Haughley, Suffolk
Mr Isaac James Moore
Sue and Barry Moore, Haughley, Suffolk
Eric J. Noy, Haughley, Suffolk
Ronald J. Nunn, Haughley, Suffolk
Derrick P. Paddy, Haughley, Suffolk
Darran Paddy, Bixby Avenue, Haughley
Brian and Sue Palmer, Mendlesham, Suffolk
Eric and Jenny Palmer, Haughley New Street, Suffolk
K.W.R.V. Palmer, Haughley, Suffolk
John 'Tinker' Parker
Canon Deirdre Parmenter
Olive and George Parry, Haughley
Woody Perrett-Jones, Haughley, Suffolk
The Philpot Family, Haughley

Miss Ann Heather Pryke, Haughley, Suffolk
Gemma R. Puricelli, Wallington, Surrey
Ernie, Rachel, Kim, Samantha, and Louise Rabett, Haughley
The Ranson Family, Haughley, Suffolk
Frederick Rapsey, Walnutree Manor, Haughley Green
Lisa M. Ratcliffe, Haughley, Suffolk
Mr Melvin Redit, Haughley Green, Suffolk
Gill Robinson (née Brand), Harleston, Stowmarket
Des Rolfe, Battisford, Suffolk
D.P. Rutherford, Haughley, Suffolk
Lee R. Shave, Haughley, Suffolk
Chris Spink, Ipswich, Suffolk
Dennis and Gwen Spink, Haughley, Suffolk
Gordon Seymour Stiff
Neil Talbot, Elmswell, Suffolk
Shirley Talbot, Haughley, Suffolk
Alan Taylor, Reigate, Surrey
Colin Taylor, Normandy, Guildford, Surrey
C.F. Taylor, Old Newton
Nesta Taylor, Haughley Green, Suffolk
Derek and Enid Thompson, Haughley, Suffolk
Drs Helen and Gordon Thomson, Bacton Green
Marina J. Thorpe, Haughley, Suffolk
Mr J.R. Turner, Worcester
John F.W. Walling, Newton Abbot, Devon
Trevor B. Waspe, Great Finborough, Suffolk
A. Watson, Haughley, Suffolk
Pauline A. Watts, Princes Risborough, Buckinghamshire
Pamela Welburn, Stowmarket, Suffolk
Rosemary Welburn, Haughley, Suffolk
Mr and Mrs S.R. Wells, Haughley, Suffolk
John and Margaret White, Haughley Green
Mr Manfred White, Stafford
Marjorie Williams (née King), Stowmarket, Suffolk
Steve Williams, Stowmarket, Suffolk
Hugh and Marion Wilson, Haughley, Suffolk

✦ FURTHER TITLES ✦

Community Histories

The Book of Addiscombe • Canning and Clyde Road Residents Association and Friends
The Book of Addiscombe, Vol. II • Canning and Clyde Road Residents Association and Friends
The Book of Ashburton • Stuart Hands and Pete Webb
The Book of Axminster with Kilmington • Les Berry and Gerald Gosling
Bakewell • Trevor Brighton
The Book of Bampton • Caroline Seward
The Book of Barnstaple • Avril Stone
The Book of Barnstaple, Vol. II • Avril Stone
The Book of The Bedwyns • Bedwyn History Society
The Book of Bergh Apton • Geoffrey I. Kelly
The Book of Bickington • Stuart Hands
The Book of Bideford • Peter Christie and Alison Grant
Blandford Forum: A Millennium Portrait • Blandford Forum Town Council
The Book of Boscastle • Rod and Anne Knight
The Book of Bourton-on-the-Hill, Batsford and Sezincote • Allen Firth
The Book of Bramford • Bramford Local History Group
The Book of Breage & Germoe • Stephen Polglase
The Book of Bridestowe • D. Richard Cann
The Book of Bridport • Rodney Legg
The Book of Brixham • Frank Pearce
The Book of Buckfastleigh • Sandra Coleman
The Book of Buckland Monachorum & Yelverton • Pauline Hamilton-Leggett
The Book of Budleigh Salterton • D. Richard Cann
The Book of Carharrack • Carharrack Old Cornwall Society
The Book of Carshalton • Stella Wilks and Gordon Rookledge
The Parish Book of Cerne Abbas • Vivian and Patricia Vale
The Book of Chagford • Iain Rice
The Book of Chapel-en-le-Frith • Mike Smith
The Book of Chittlehamholt with Warkleigh & Satterleigh • Richard Lethbridge
The Book of Chittlehampton • Various
The Book of Codford • Romy Wyeth
The Book of Colney Heath • Bryan Lilley
The Book of Constantine • Moore and Trethowan
The Book of Cornwood and Lutton • Compiled by the People of the Parish
The Book of Crediton • John Heal
The Book of Creech St Michael • June Small
The Book of Crowcombe, Bicknoller and Sampford Brett • Maurice and Joyce Chidgey
The Book of Crudwell • Tony Pain
The Book of Cullompton • Compiled by the People of the Parish
The Book of Dawlish • Frank Pearce
The Book of Dulverton, Brushford, Bury & Exebridge • Dulverton and District Civic Society
The Book of Dunster • Hilary Binding
The Book of Easton • Easton Village History Project
The Book of Edale • Gordon Miller
The Ellacombe Book • Sydney R. Langmead
The Book of Exmouth • W.H. Pascoe
The Book of Grampound with Creed • Bane and Oliver
The Book of Gosport • Lesley Burton and Brian Musselwhite
The Book of Haughley • Howard Stephens
The Book of Hayle • Harry Pascoe
The Book of Hayling Island & Langstone • Peter Rogers
The Book of Helston • Jenkin with Carter
The Book of Hemyock • Clist and Dracott
The Book of Herne Hill • Patricia Jenkyns
The Book of Hethersett • Hethersett Society Research Group
The Book of High Bickington • Avril Stone
The Book of Honiton • Gerald Gosling
The Book of Ilsington • Dick Wills
The Book of Kingskerswell • Carsewella Local History Group
The Book of Lamerton • Ann Cole and Friends
Lanner, A Cornish Mining Parish • Sharron Schwartz and Roger Parker
The Book of Leigh & Bransford • Malcolm Scott
The Second Book of Leigh & Bransford • Malcolm Scott
The Book of Litcham with Lexham & Mileham • Litcham Historical and Amenity Society
The Book of Llangain • Haydyn Williams
The Book of Loddiswell • Loddiswell Parish History Group
The New Book of Lostwithiel • Barbara Fraser
The Book of Lulworth • Rodney Legg
The Book of Lustleigh • Joe Crowdy
The Book of Lydford • Compiled by Barbara Weeks
The Book of Lyme Regis • Rodney Legg
The Book of Manaton • Compiled by the People of the Parish

THE BOOK OF HAUGHLEY

The Book of Markyate • Markyate Local History Society
The Book of Mawnan • Mawnan Local History Group
The Book of Meavy • Pauline Hemery
The Book of Mere • Dr David Longbourne
The Book of Minehead with Alcombe • Binding and Stevens
The Book of Monks Orchard and Eden Park • Ian Muir and Pat Manning
The Book of Morchard Bishop • Jeff Kingaby
The Book of Mylor • Mylor Local History Group
The Book of Narborough • Narborough Local History Society
The Book of Newdigate • John Callcut
The Book of Newtown • Keir Foss
The Book of Nidderdale • Nidderdale Museum Society
The Book of Northlew with Ashbury • Northlew History Group
The Book of North Newton • J.C. and K.C. Robins
The Book of North Tawton • Baker, Hoare and Shields
The Book of Nynehead • Nynehead & District History Society
The Book of Okehampton • Roy and Ursula Radford
The Book of Ottery St Mary • Gerald Gosling and Peter Harris
The Book of Paignton • Frank Pearce
The Book of Penge, Anerley & Crystal Palace • Peter Abbott
The Book of Peter Tavy with Cudlipptown • Peter Tavy Heritage Group
The Book of Pimperne • Jean Coull
The Book of Plymtree • Tony Eames
The Book of Poole • Rodney Legg
The Book of Porlock • Dennis Corner
Postbridge – The Heart of Dartmoor • Reg Bellamy
The Book of Priddy • Albert Thompson
The Book of Princetown • Dr Gardner-Thorpe
The Book of Probus • Alan Kent and Danny Merrifield
The Book of Rattery • By the People of the Parish
The Book of Roadwater, Leighland and Treborough • Clare and Glyn Court
The Book of St Austell • Peter Hancock
The Book of St Day • Joseph Mills and Paul Annear
The Book of St Dennis and Goss Moor • Kenneth Rickard
The Book of St Levan • St Levan Local History Group
The Book of Sampford Courtenay with Honeychurch • Stephanie Pouya
The Book of Sculthorpe • Gary Windeler

The Book of Seaton • Ted Gosling
The Book of Sidmouth • Ted Gosling and Sheila Luxton
The Book of Silverton • Silverton Local History Society
The Book of South Molton • Jonathan Edmunds
The Book of South Stoke with Midford • Edited by Robert Parfitt
South Tawton & South Zeal with Sticklepath • Roy and Ursula Radford
The Book of Sparkwell with Hemerdon & Lee Mill • Pam James
The Book of Staverton • Pete Lavis
The Book of Stithians • Stithians Parish History Group
The Book of Stogumber, Monksilver, Nettlecombe & Elworthy • Maurice and Joyce Chidgey
The Book of South Brent • Greg Wall
The Book of Studland • Rodney Legg
The Book of Swanage • Rodney Legg
The Book of Tavistock • Gerry Woodcock
The Book of Thorley • Sylvia McDonald and Bill Hardy
The Book of Torbay • Frank Pearce
The Book of Truro • Christine Parnell
The Book of Uplyme • Gerald Gosling and Jack Thomas
The Book of Watchet • Compiled by David Banks
The Book of Wendling, Longham and Beeston with Bittering • Stephen Olley
The Book of West Huntspill • By the People of the Parish
The Book of Weston-super-Mare • Sharon Poole
The Book of Whitchurch • Gerry Woodcock
Widecombe-in-the-Moor • Stephen Woods
Widecombe – Uncle Tom Cobley & All • Stephen Woods
The Book of Williton • Michael Williams
The Book of Wincanton • Rodney Legg
The Book of Winscombe • Margaret Tucker
The Book of Witheridge • Peter and Freda Tout and John Usmar
The Book of Withycombe • Chris Boyles
Woodbury: The Twentieth Century Revisited • Roger Stokes
The Book of Woolmer Green • Compiled by the People of the Parish
The Book of Yetminster • Shelagh Hill

For details of any of the above titles or if you are interested in writing your own history, please contact: Commissioning Editor, Community Histories, Halsgrove House, Lower Moor Way, Tiverton, Devon EX16 6SS, England; email: katyc@halsgrove.com